COSTA RICA

COSTA RICA
THE FORESTS OF EDEN

KEVIN SCHAFER

RIZZOLI
NEW YORK

First published in the United
States of America in 1996 by
Rizzoli International
Publications, Inc.
300 Park Avenue South
New York, New York 10010

Library of Congress Cataloging-
in-Publication Data

Schafer, Kevin.
      Costa Rica : the forests of Eden / Kevin Schafer
             p. cm.
      Includes bibliographical references
      ISBN 0-8478-1984-1 (hc)
      1. National parks and reserves—Costa Rica
      2. Natural history — Costa Rica
      3. National parks and reserves — Costa Rica—Pictorial works. I Title.
SB484.C8S33 1996
508.7286—dc20   96-19095
                                            CIP

Designed by Joseph Guglietti
Printed and bound in Italy

ACKNOWLEDGMENTS

As with any project of this scope, this book could never have been completed without the generous help of a large number of people. No one provided more logistical help than Tamara Budowski and Maria Consuelo Leon of Horizontes, the premier travel company in Costa Rica. They watched over us and simply made things happen in the most miraculous ways during the long months in the field. *A nos amigas muy especiales, muchas gracias y pura vida.*

We were fortunate to spend time with a variety of dedicated Costa Rican naturalists and guides on our journeys, men and women who helped us find things of interest, carried equipment, and shared long days in the field. Deserving special mention are Alexander Villegas at the Monteverde Conservation League, Jaime Alvarado at Selva Verde, Roy Arroyo at Hacienda La Amistad, and Geovanny Bogarriny at the Arenal Observatory Lodge. Their knowledge and experience made my job much easier—and much more fun. I would also like to thank Stanley Arguedas and Luis Mena of the Cabo Blanco Reserve for their enthusiasm and fine company.

Both Alvaro Ugalde and Mario Boza gave generously of their time to answer my questions and to both I am very grateful. At the same time, to thank them for their contributions to conservation both past and present seems woefully inadequate. I hope that this book will reveal some of what they have helped save for all of us. In addition, there are many other hardworking and dedicated people throughout the national park system, and the various other government organizations, public and private, who have made vital contributions toward protecting Costa Rican biodiversity. We are all in their debt.

Sven-Olof Lindblad of Special Expeditions in New York has, over a number of years, provided significant support to make this book a reality. I am grateful, too, for help from David Carr of the Caribbean Conservation Corporation, Fernando Bermudez of the National Parks Service, Hernan and Mario Posla of Butterfly Paradise, and LACSA Airlines. A special thanks should also go to both Steven Lill of Casa Corcovado and Jim Zook, birder extraordinaire.

Valuable help also came from Gary Hartshorn, Chris Wille and Diane Jukovsky, Ingrid Ayub, Richard and Margot Frisius of Amigos de las Aves, Luis and Judy Arroyo of Aviarios de Caribe, Efrain Chacon of Albergue Savegre, Hacienda Baru, Kathryn Stoner and Mauricio Quesada, and the Costa Rican Tourist Board, who provided considerable support for this project.

Special thanks go to Teresa Sharp, who kept things together at home during our long months on the road, and helped this project along in a variety of important ways.

I am especially indebted to Manuela Soares, my editor at Rizzoli, who believed in this project from the beginning and was its faithful advocate throughout.

I must also acknowledge the contributions of Edward Schafer, my father, who first introduced me to the rainforests of Central America. A Chinese scholar and tropical birder, he loved Costa Rica and traveled there many times. I wish he had lived to see this book, because it is partly his.

Finally, no one deserves more credit for the idea and completion of this book than my wife Marty, careful editor, fine artist, and top-notch field companion, who shared nearly every part of its creation and gave me the confidence to take it on. I will always feel fortunate to have found such a wonderful partner, in work and in life.

FOR MARTY

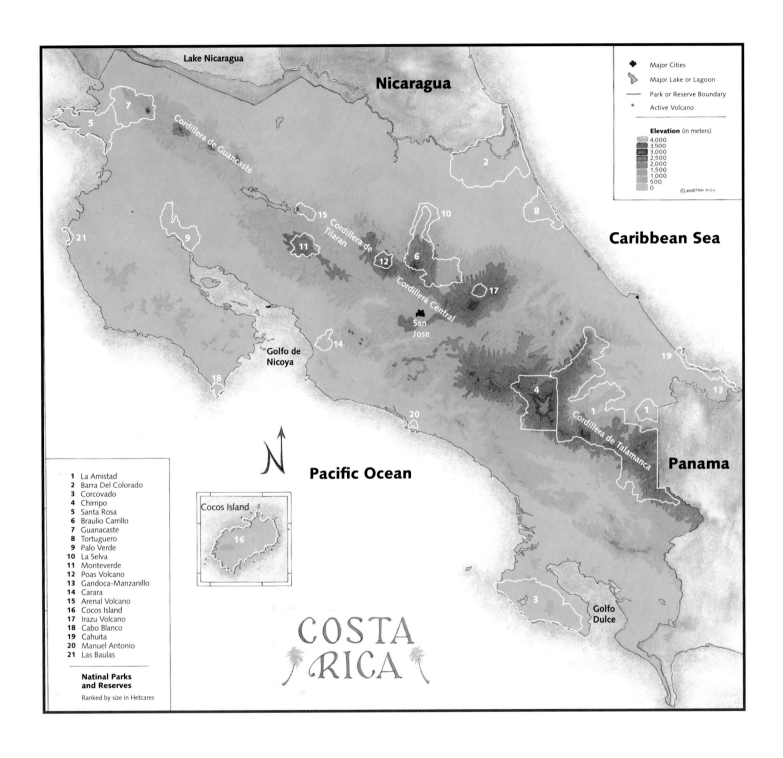

Lake Nicaragua

Nicaragua

Cordillera de Guancaste

Caribbean Sea

Cordillera de Tilaran

Cordillera Central

San Jose

Golfo de Nicoya

Cordillera de Talamanca

Panama

N

Pacific Ocean

Cocos Island

Golfo Dulce

COSTA RICA

	Major Cities
	Major Lake or Lagoon
—	Park or Reserve Boundary
•	Active Volcano

Elevation (in meters)
4,000
3,500
3,000
2,500
2,000
1,500
1,000
500
0

©MARTHA HILL

1 La Amistad
2 Barra Del Colorado
3 Corcovado
4 Chirripo
5 Santa Rosa
6 Braulio Carrillo
7 Guanacaste
8 Tortuguero
9 Palo Verde
10 La Selva
11 Monteverde
12 Poas Volcano
13 Gandoca-Manzanillo
14 Carara
15 Arenal Volcano
16 Cocos Island
17 Irazu Volcano
18 Cabo Blanco
19 Cahuita
20 Manuel Antonio
21 Las Baulas

Natinal Parks and Reserves

Ranked by size in Hetcares

CONTENTS

8   FOREWORD

12   INTRODUCTION

16   **JAGUARS ON THE BEACH**
THE PACIFIC COAST

46   **MOUNTAINS OF FIRE**
THE VOLCANIC CORDILLERA

72   **THE UNTIRING SUN**
THE DRY NORTHWEST

102   **EYES IN THE WATER**
THE CARIBBEAN COAST

132   **THE FORESTS OF EDEN**
THE TALAMANCA RANGE

158   AFTERWORD

160   BIBLIOGRAPHY

FOREWORD

A SHORT WHILE AGO, A WOMAN from one of the American conservation organizations visited me. As we were talking, she mentioned how refreshing it was to speak to an optimist. "Yes," I said, "in Costa Rica, we are optimists. We couldn't have put together such a marvelous system of national parks without it." And by continuing to do so, the country is turning the tide in favor of nature and of future generations.

People are inclined to follow the lead of the winners and the visionaries. What they share are optimism, determination, and hard work. During the last twenty-five years Costa Rica has been applying these qualities to the job of saving and putting to wise use its extraordinary biological diversity.

For a country as small as ours, this natural resource is a mixed blessing. On the one hand, it is an unparalleled wealth of species whose benefits to mankind are yet to be explored. On the other hand, it is an enormous burden, a global responsibility way beyond the country's present economic means.

Some think that we Costa Ricans have made a risky choice. For a poor country, investing so much in the establishment and protection of ecosystems might appear foolhardy. Luckily, investing in ecosystems is being taken seriously by the world at large, and Costa Rica, like other countries committed to conservation, feels justified in its efforts.

Creating a system of national parks forced Costa Rica to look at the future in much the same way our ancestors did when they eliminated militarism and made education the national priority. Costa Rica has undertaken to demonstrate that conservation is essential if we are to achieve sustainability, and if we care to be remembered by future generations with some respect.

In addition to being a steward for nearly 5 percent of the entire planet's biodiversity, Costa Rica is also a little experiment, with worldwide implications, in the search for different ways of behaving as a society—ways we hope will allow us to live and progress in harmony, as individuals and as nations, and still maintain true options for our children.

Today in Costa Rica the concept of ecosystems is seen with more respect. After all, they are not only very beautiful, but they provide our water and energy needs, and contribute other national and global benefits. At the same time, tourists from all over the world seem to love them. Protected ecosystems are now bringing more foreign exchange to the country than bananas or coffee.

And here is where the paradox begins to make sense. There seem to be ways of doing things which are not only environmentally friendly, but economically very productive. If this continues to be true, the tide will keep turning in favor of protecting Costa Rica's natural wealth.

Kevin Schafer has created an extraordinarily beautiful book. In it, he not only conveys a true feeling of the wonders that inhabit our national parks and reserves, but also the human drama and optimism that created them, and that, today, continues to support and improve them.

As I was reading *Costa Rica: The Forests of Eden*, I enjoyed being able to revisit most of my national parks through the superb photography and excellent text. In particular, I think those readers who care about nature and who have visited or hope to visit the parks in person will find that this book definitely whets the appetite!

ALVARO UGALDE
Former Director
National Parks of Costa Rica

INTRODUCTION

WHEN I FIRST TRAVELED to Costa Rica more than a decade ago, as one of a group of journalists, I knew very little about the country, or about the things we would see. During the next two weeks, I found myself hiking deep into the rain forest, peering into the mouth of an active volcano, and sitting, enthralled, as sea turtles dragged themselves from the sea to lay their eggs. Costa Rica, I discovered, was a quite remarkable place.

No bigger than the state of West Virginia, with a population of just over three million, Costa Rica is a largely agricultural nation, a major producer of bananas and coffee. Despite its location in a part of the world rife with political unrest, Costa Rica remains a striking anomaly, both peaceful and democratic.

Having abolished its army in 1949, Costa Rica freed itself from the enormous financial and political drain that maintenance of a large military can often entail. It redirected its resources, instead, toward education and social services, creating a better standard of living for its people than in any other country in the region. Despite these accomplishments, Costa Rica was still little known to the outside world until 1987, when then-president Oscar Arias was awarded the Nobel Prize for his efforts to bring peace to Central America. Suddenly people began to take notice.

All along, however, Costa Rica had been quietly making a name for itself in a very different sphere—as a bold pioneer in environmental protection. In the past twenty-five years, this small country has created an extraordinary network of national parks and reserves that today rivals that of any country on earth. In all, these parks encompass more than 12 percent of Costa Rican territory, with important new areas still being added every year. By any measure, this is a remarkable achievement, but especially for a relatively poor nation struggling toward economic development.

When Costa Rica's park system was created in the late 1960s, the world environmental movement was still in its infancy. At the time, Costa Rica had one of the fastest growing populations in the hemisphere, and a distinctly dismal record of land use; in the years following World War II, more than half of its tropical forests had been cut down. As a result, a handful of Costa Ricans began to realize that this rapid deforestation threatened to transform their country, once lush and beautiful, into little more than a cattle pasture.

In response, they set out to protect something of this natural beauty before it vanished forever, a victim of the chainsaw and the plow. In 1969 a National Park Service was created as a vehicle for land protection. Many people were involved in this effort: biologists, landowners, government officials, and conservationists. Several Costa Rican presidential administrations made important additions to the park system during their tenure and committed considerable funds for the system's growth and protection when it was expensive, politically and financially, to do so.

From its very beginning the national park system of Costa Rica has been different from those in many other countries —including the United States. Rather than being seen simply as recreational and scenic treasures for human benefit, as were most of the early national parks in the United States, Costa Rican parks have largely been planned to protect the plants and animals that inhabit them. Many of these parks are remote and inaccessible, with no campgrounds, no visitor centers, and, in some cases, no trails. The emphasis has been, instead, on protecting biological communities for their own sake.

This emphasis on living ecosystems stems directly from the fact that many of the key figures in the development of the Costa Rican park system were biologists and conservationists. Among these were two men who, perhaps more than any others, devoted their lives to the creation of national parks in Costa Rica, and in doing so, transformed the face of the entire country.

One of these was Mario Boza, who served as the first director of the National Park Service. In 1968 Boza was a twenty-seven-year-old graduate of the University of Costa Rica, where he had trained to be an agronomist. During a visit that year to the United States, he found himself deeply impressed by the possibilities of national parks, both as a framework for land protection, and as a potential source of revenue. He also looked at the income that tourism had brought to places like East Africa, and believed that a system of parks could be similarly successful in Costa Rica.

For his master's thesis, Boza prepared a proposal on how a Costa Rican park could be designed and operated. A year later, when the park service came into being, his paper formed the basis for the first national park, Poas Volcano.

The other key figure in the growth and consolidation of the fledgling park service was Alvaro Ugalde. At the time that the park service began, Ugalde was a biology student, wondering what to do after he finished his studies. Then, in 1970, he was enlisted by Boza to manage the new Santa Rosa National Park, which was facing serious opposition from surrounding landowners and problems with squatters. In 1974, Ugalde took over from Boza as director of the entire system, a position he would hold for the next twelve years.

Boza and Ugalde are often referred to as the fathers of Costa Rica's national parks system. Although many others deserve to share the credit for creating the remarkable system, both Boza and Ugalde were indispensable advocates in the early years, when parks had few funds and faced enormous setbacks. Their perspectives on the evolution of parks in Costa Rica are included throughout this book.

Today, Costa Rica has become something of a household name, a place almost synonymous with rainforest conservation. The reputation is well deserved, and has been rewarded with increasing numbers of visitors every year from all over the world. In 1994, for the first time, tourism surpassed bananas as the nation's chief source of revenue.

Peter Raven, director of the Missouri Botanical Garden, has described the creation of Costa Rica's national park system as "one of the great accomplishments of the human race over the last thirty years." The success of Costa Rica's parks has set a standard for the rest of the world, both in the effective preservation of its natural resources, and in making conservation a keystone of its economic strategy. In this, Costa Rica has given us all a most precious commodity—renewed hope for the earth's future.

For many years, I had wanted to devote an extended period of time to capturing something of the natural beauty of Costa Rica on film—its spectacular landscapes and dazzling array of wildlife. The photographs included in this book are the product of five intensive expeditions made between October 1994 and November 1995. During that time my wife, Marty, and I traveled the length of the country several times, appreciating for the first time how big, and how startlingly diverse, it really is. We visited most of the major parks and reserves, but inevitably missed others; happily, there are simply so many protected areas in this small country that few people, including most Costa Ricans, could ever hope to visit them all.

The work complete, I now realize with some humility that I have only scratched the surface. To include it all would easily be a lifetime's work. This, then, should not be regarded as an exhaustive catalog of everything Costa Rica has to offer, but a glimpse of a splendid corner of the earth.

This book is divided into five chapters based on Costa Rica's major geographic regions: the Pacific Coast, the arid Northwest, the Caribbean lowlands, the Volcanic Cordillera; and the Talamanca Range. Within each chapter I have tried to convey a sense of the unique features of that region, the natural histo-ry of some of the living things found there, and some information about the national parks that help protect them. I have not touched on the country's long human history; I am a naturalist at heart and my bias shows.

Finally, a brief caution. There is something unavoidably deceptive in a collection of photographs of this sort, since it may create an expectation that the forest is teeming with wild creatures. With experienced guides, extraordinary luck, and enormous patience, you may be fortunate enough to see some of them. But if you do not see a jaguar on your first visit—or your fourth—don't despair; there are many Costa Ricans who have spent many years of their lives in the field and have never seen a wild jaguar. Simply be thankful that jaguars, and sloths, and even leaf-cutter ants still wander these forests at all. Ultimately, it is for them that the national parks were created, as much as for ourselves.

JAGUARS ON THE BEACH

THE PACIFIC COAST

THE TROPICAL RAIN FOREST does not howl or shriek, it buzzes. In the heart of Corcovado National Park, the windless shadows of the forest floor throb with the rhythmic humming of cicadas, as if the air itself were sizzling in the heat. Nothing is moving, yet everywhere there is life.

This is not a place of vivid spectacle, but of nuance and detail—an endless stream of army ants sweeping across the trail; the sharp "crack" of a male manakin, snapping his wings to lure a passing female; or a tiny frog, the color of fallen leaves, sitting motionless among the litter, praying to go unnoticed.

With roughly eight hundred kilometers of rocky headlands, beaches, and offshore islands, Costa Rica's Pacific coast is one of the most spectacular shorelines on earth. Less than a generation ago most of this coast was uninhabited, but new roads and new hotels are quickly transforming it from wilderness to a long string of popular beach resorts.

However, there are still a handful of places where the natural landscape has prevailed—one of them is Corcovado National Park. Located on the isolated Osa Peninsula, Corcovado is the last large expanse of coastal rain forest left along the entire Pacific coast of Central America. There are four hundred species of birds found here, six thousand species of insects described so far and five hundred types of trees, roughly two-thirds the number found in all of North America.

Although these numbers imply a kind of biological richness, they only hint at the scale of wilderness within Corcovado's boundaries. For me, there exists a far more compelling symbol—jaguars still live here. Among the rarest of rain forest creatures, jaguars are all but extinct elsewhere in Central America, their habitat dissected, the deer and wild pigs that compose their diet decimated by hunting. But in Corcovado there have been persistent sightings of something that may no longer be possible anywhere else on earth—a female jaguar and her cub, walking carelessly down an ocean beach, between forest and surf. It is a vision of a tropical Eden, timeless and eternal.

Far from cities and highways, and offering no viable port, Corcovado has been blessed by its own obscurity. It has avoided the tide of Pacific coast development; even today, there are no roads into Corcovado. To get there it is necessary to travel by boat—on days when the surf is not too high—or by chartering a small plane into a remote grass strip carved out of the jungle. Otherwise, the visitor must hoist a backpack and walk.

Corcovado has a special place in Costa Rica's park system, not because it is the largest of the parks, nor even the first, but because it is symbolic of everything that the system was designed to protect. It is physically beautiful, biologically rich, and large enough to provide a habitat for many animals that have vanished elsewhere. Besides the jaguar, Corcovado is one of the last refuges for the scarlet macaw, the Baird's tapir, the American crocodile, and a number of other desperately endangered species.

At the same time, Corcovado is also a kind of spiritual Mecca for the tropical biologist, a place on a par with the wildest corners of the Amazon. The forest here grows on a mythic scale—giant trees that have never known the sound of a saw and waterfalls that drop from primeval forest directly into the surf. There are almost certainly plants and animals in these forests that are still to be discovered.

For the nonscientist, however, it can be difficult to fully appreciate all this biological wealth. To most of us, one rainforest looks superficially like another. The trees may be taller in one area, or the understory more open (as is often the case in unlogged primary forests), but otherwise the distinctions are often too subtle for the untrained eye. It is a messy environment, a chaos of green.

Powerful and secretive, there is no more compelling symbol of the tropical forest than the jaguar.

Clockwise from upper left: A red-lored amazon parrot reaches for a ripe guava fruit; incubating its eggs, a tody-flycatcher peers from its hanging nest; on Cabo Blanco Island, a brown booby pants to dissipate body heat; a yellow-bellied elaenia sits motionless on a nest made of lichens and twigs.

Only in the company of a specialist can you begin to appreciate some of the differences—the astonishing diversity of trees, the variety of bird calls, or the presence of an utterly new kind of insect, unknown to science. But it does not require a specialist to appreciate the stories any tropical forest has to tell.

One of the most remarkable animals of the rainforest is also one of its most humble—the leaf-cutter ant. A short walk on any of Corcovado's trails will quickly reveal what appears to be a parade of green leaf fragments, marching along the forest floor. It is a foraging party of leaf-cutter ants, returning to their nest with the bits of leaves and flowers they have spent the day gathering among the trees of the forest.

Leaf-cutters do not eat the leaves they carry. Instead, after being deposited deep in the subterranean chambers that make up the ants' nest, the leaves are chewed and mixed with ant droppings. In this rich mulch grows a kind of fungus, known only from these nests and unable to reproduce without the ants' help; it is upon this fungus that the ants feed.

This much of the story is well documented, but as is so typical of tropical ecosystems, there is still much more that we do not know. How, for example, do the ants choose their trees? Leaf-cutters are clearly very selective about what they gather; while there may be hundreds of leafy trees close to their nest, foraging parties may travel a kilometer or more in search of their next victim. And when they find a tree they like, they may only take a few leaves—or strip it bare. It is as though they work from a kind of recipe—a few leaves of Cecropia, a dash of crabwood, and chew lightly. But if the ants are working from a recipe, how are the details of that recipe—the ingredients and amounts—transmitted from one ant to another? How do they know when they have enough of one kind of tree and that it is time to move to another? We simply have no idea.

It is our rudimentary understanding of even such commonplace events that makes the tropical forest so eternally fascinating to biologists—and holds out real hope of profound scientific discovery. Knowing more about the leaf-cutter ants, for example, could reveal something new about chemical communication, or the medicinal properties of plants. Key breakthroughs are almost certainly contained within such bizarre and complicated interactions of plants and animals, between predators and prey, between host and parasite.

In the 1960s, after a number of researchers conducted the first systematic biological surveys in Corcovado, it became clear that it was a remarkable place in vital need of protection. Almost as soon as the park service was created, many proposed that Corcovado be added to the system, and it became so by presidential decree on October 31, 1975.

With its creation as a park, however, the problems at Corcovado were only just beginning. For although the park was now law, the land was not unoccupied, and within a few years a major struggle would pit the ideals of conservation against political and economic realities.

Alvaro Ugalde, then director of the park service, remembers what he and his staff were up against. "Half of what is now the park was owned by a North American forestry company and the land was filled with squatters. The Costa Rican government had to buy out and relocate 166 families who were living in the park area." But evicting people from their homes is neither easy, nor popular. In the end, the process took over a year to accomplish, and cost almost two million dollars.

By 1978 the squatters were gone—but the problems were still not over. For fifty years, small amounts of gold had been taken out of the Osa Peninsula by *oreros*—gold miners—working the streams and rivers in the southern part of Corcovado. By the early 1980s the

Left:

Its skin the color of fallen leaves, the fer-de-lance is a rare sight, although it is the most common venomous snake in Costa Rica.

Opposite:

Roosting in the dense tangle of the canopy, a spectacled owl waits for night.

number of miners had risen dramatically. "At one time there were fifteen hundred miners living within the park," Ugalde remembers. "It was like the Wild West, with miners, prostitutes, and everything." Even worse, these new squatters were cutting the forest and hunting for game. When a team of biologists surveyed the mining area in 1985, they reported that there were almost no animals left, and that rivers and streams were fouled with mining debris and human waste—all within the confines of the national park.

Convinced that the park was being destroyed, Ugalde spent the next six months trying to convince ministers and government agencies to let him do something about it. Finally, in early 1986, armed with a court order, the Rural Guard was called in to arrest the miners and move them out forcibly. Once the miners were moved, the government spent several million dollars helping them find alternative ways of making a living.

Corcovado's birth was among the most traumatic in the park system's history. By contrast, Manuel Antonio National Park, one hundred kilometers north along the Pacific coast came about much more easily. Created three years before Corcovado, Manuel Antonio is today one of the most popular parks in Costa Rica, especially among the Costa Ricans themselves. It is also one of the smallest.

Named for an early colonial figure, Manuel Antonio is situated on a spectacular stretch of the coast where rocky headlands are separated by long promenades of perfect white sand. Rising above the beaches is a remnant slice of rainforest, filled with monkeys and other animals in numbers surprising for a park its size.

According to Ugalde, the creation of this park involved little of the protracted struggle that marked the fight for Corcovado. "The land at Manuel Antonio had been purchased by some Americans and Canadians, who put a gate across the entrance to the beach and started selling lots. But this was an area that had been used by the people in the community for many years, and they started complaining and burning the gates—and it grew into a big conflict. And we, like vultures looking for opportunities, went there and saw the area and said, 'My God, this should be a national park!'

"So we went through the town with a car and loudspeakers, saying so. Then the congressmen from the area spoke up in congress—and within weeks there was a national park. Even today, we still owe the money for about 35 percent of the land to a local wealthy family. We haven't paid them, and thank God they're not asking to be paid!"

In recent years, however, with an unprecedented boom in tourism, Manuel Antonio has become a victim of its own popularity. During school breaks and national holidays, the beaches at Manuel Antonio are often jammed with people, while jet skis roar back and forth offshore. Traffic jams clog the narrow road that ends at the entrance to the park, where young hustlers extort money to "guard" your car.

Still, Manuel Antonio has undeniable treasures. Among other things, it is one of the last places on earth to see the Central American squirrel monkey, which is perilously close to extinction. It is perhaps also the best place in Costa Rica to see a three-toed sloth, that odd, slow-moving denizen of the treetops.

In Costa Rica, the sloth is known simply as the *perezoso*, or "lazy one." Most of the time, it is virtually impossible to see. Sloths spend their days curled up in the top of a tree, looking like little more than a clump of dried leaves. Their chief activity, apparently, is sleeping; only occasionally do they summon the energy necessary to initiate the search for food.

Sloths are multiplying quickly in the forests of Manuel Antonio, largely because there is no one to prevent them from doing so. Small and isolated from

Keel-billed toucans are noisy, social birds, using their extravagant bills to gobble down everything from fruit to frogs—and even other birds' eggs.

Overleaf:
A brown booby glides above its own reflection mirrored in the sea near Cocos Island.

other forest by miles of open country, Manuel Antonio is too small to maintain top predators, especially the harpy eagle, the sloth's natural enemy. As a result, sloths have little to fear and plenty to eat. In fact, the only thing that keeps them from overwhelming the forest altogether is the amount of available food.

Research on sloths in Panama suggests that they are among the most abundant mammals (other than bats) in the rainforest—as many as eight adults may share a single hectare. One reason they can coexist in such close quarters is that individual sloths tend to favor specific species of trees, passing on that preference to their young. For that reason, sloths with different specialties can maintain overlapping ranges, happily avoiding competition with their neighbors.

A sloth is a peculiar creature in any number of ways, but in one specific behavior, it is downright mysterious. For some reason the sloth—a perfectly designed arboreal animal—invariably descends from the safety of the treetops once a week and digs a small hole in which to deposit its feces. Thirty minutes later, the job done, he climbs—always slowly—back up to the canopy.

Such a laborious process clearly exposes the sloth to ground-based predators, so there surely must be some compelling advantage for him to do it or else the behavior would quickly be driven from the genetic pool. The only trouble is, no one can figure out how the sloth benefits. Some observers have suggested that the sloth is attempting to nourish its host trees by fertilizing their roots. Anything carelessly dropped onto the forest floor from above would likely be eaten by decomposers long before it added much nourishment to the soil, but by burying their waste close to the roots, sloths may be trying to maximize its benefit.

Whatever the reason behind this odd behavior, the tree is not the only beneficiary. There are many species of moths, beetles,

Opposite:

Palm leaves create a striking geometry in Carara National Park.

Right, above:

Massive trees and heavy lines, Corcovado.

Center:

The flower of a bromeliad adds a splash of color to the forest interior, Esquinas National Park.

Below:

Light and shadow play in the forest understory, Carara.

Left:

Tropical animals have elaborate strategies for avoiding predation. The waxy growths on this insect's back may lure a predator away from more vital tissue.

Opposite:

Zanthoxylum trees have formidable spines to discourage climbing herbivores.

and mites that make use of this weekly event. All live their entire lives among the thick fur of the three-toed sloth, and for each of them, this regular visit to the forest floor is an essential part of their life history. The only way they can reproduce is by hopping off the sloth while he's on the ground and laying their eggs in his waste. Then, after feeding happily underground, the next generation of insects emerge as adults at the surface and set off in search of their own sloth, completing the cycle.

While Manuel Antonio ranks as one of Costa Rica's most visited parks, far beyond its western horizon is a park few people will ever see; the rugged, cliff-lined Isla del Coco, or Cocos Island.

Cocos Island has belonged to Costa Rica since the middle of the nineteenth century, but it has remained beyond the reach of most Costa Ricans ever since. It became a national park in 1978. Over the centuries, there have been several attempts to settle the island, but with its rugged topography, thin soil, and upwards of seven meters of annual rainfall, it has defeated the ambitions of everyone who has tried to live there.

Nonetheless, with its abundant fresh water and remote location, Cocos is known to have long been a regular anchorage for pirates. Some almost certainly buried treasure here, but despite hundreds of expeditions to find it, the island has yet to give it up.

Cocos is a volcanic island, the exposed part of a submarine mountain chain that stretches from Costa Rica to the Galapagos. Because it was never connected to any mainland, every living thing found here had to travel over five hundred kilometers of open ocean.

Perhaps blown offshore during a storm, at least three kinds of birds found their way here—a cuckoo, a flycatcher, and a finch. In fact, the latter is thought to be closely related to Darwin's finch of the Galapagos, some eight hundred

kilometers to the southwest. All three of these birds are found only on Cocos and nowhere else on earth. In the language of specialists, they are endemic. Other endemics, with equally mysterious provenance, are two kinds of lizards, three species of spiders, and even some freshwater fish. All were somehow delivered to Cocos by accident over the past milennia and evolved independently from their mainland ancestors.

More than two thousand people visited Cocos in 1994, twice the number from the previous year. But by far the majority of these come not to see the Cocos finch but to dive on the most isolated—and untouched—coral reefs in all of Central America. Among diving circles, Cocos is legendary for its massive gatherings of sharks, including great circling schools of hammerheads.

Besides Cocos Island, Costa Rica has created several other marine parks. One is Cano Island, just offshore from the Osa Peninsula. Best known for its fringing reefs, Cano is also thought to have been a place sacred to pre-Columbian peoples because of the mysterious spherical stones—obviously shaped by human hand—that have been found scattered around the island.

North of Cano Island, meanwhile, is a place that holds a special niche in the history of Costa Rica's parks. On a remote point of land, at the extreme southern tip of the Nicoya Peninsula is Cabo Blanco, the White Cape. Here, the restless swells of the Pacific meet the placid water of the Gulf of Nicoya in a dramatic confrontation of waves and rugged shoreline. The cape draws its name not from the color of the forested hills that drop precipitously to the water, but from the single barren island that lies just off its tip. A colony of brown boobies on the island has left it white with generations of guano.

In some ways, it was Cabo Blanco that inspired the Costa Rican national park system, and provided the crucial

impetus for its creation. In the mid-1950s, a Swedish fruit farmer named Olof Wessberg moved to the Nicoya with his Danish wife, Karen. Settling near the southern end of the peninsula, they planted fruit trees and fell in love with the wildlife and natural beauty of their adopted home. Over the years, however, they watched as more and more people moved into the area, cutting down trees and clearing the land for pasture and crops. Of particular concern was a patch of natural forest right at the tip of the peninsula, at Cabo Blanco. The Wessbergs felt this forest should be saved along with the many animals for which it was a final hiding place.

For three years, the Wessbergs tried to enlist help in purchasing—and preserving—Cabo Blanco before the forest disappeared forever. They called on friends, wrote letters, and approached a number of prominent conservation organizations to contribute. With financial support from a variety of sources, the Costa Rican government declared Cabo Blanco a "strict nature reserve" in 1963.

As at Corcovado, Cabo Blanco was saved just in time. When the reserve was declared in 1963, there were only two hundred hectares of primary forest left, isolated in upper slopes of the cape. The rest was pasture or secondary forest. Even today the wild plum trees along the trail into the reserve show signs of the barbed wire that once connected them.

Natural regeneration has changed the cape a great deal in the last thirty years. The director at Cabo Blanco today, Stanley Arguedas, sees this process as one of the keys to Costa Rica's future. "It is important to save some areas that are still intact," he says. "But it is also important to restore others." Farmland has become forest again, and the plants and animals that saw their habitat reduced to smaller and smaller areas now have much more room to move. Still, many animals that once lived here, such

as spider monkeys and predatory cats, have vanished.

"We don't introduce animals because we don't know if the conditions exist yet for their survival. A forest is like a jigsaw puzzle; each animal, each plant, each insect is a piece of this puzzle, dependent on one another." In time, and when conditions are right, Arguedas hopes that as the forest is allowed to expand, some animals may find their own way back. There have been recent signs it may already be happening. In the past year, wild peccaries—gone from Cabo Blanco for decades—were seen by a farmer just north of the reserve. Arguedas was thrilled; the farmer, however, was unimpressed—the pigs were eating his beans. "It may take two hundred to three hundred years for the forest here to become a mature, primary forest in equilibrium," Arguedas says. "I won't be here to see it, but I will have been part of its history."

Although trained as an architect and chemical engineer, Arguedas has clearly found his life's work in the parks. "Unless you work for a better world, there's no reason for living. There's no point in working just for money. I'm working for the conservation of the planet." One afternoon I followed Arguedas on his rounds through the forest at Cabo Blanco. It was a slow journey, for we were constantly stopping and ducking to avoid breaking the many spider webs that stretched across the trail. (In places, the forest seems so papered with webs that it seems a miracle any flying insect could survive the night.) In this simple, careful act, I saw the mark of a new attitude alive in Costa Rica, an attitude of balancing our own needs with those of other living things.

Left:

A tiny insect hides beneath the umbrella of a translucent fungus.

Opposite:

Exquisitely fragile, the Sobralia orchid lasts only a day and then withers.

MOUNTAINS OF FIRE
THE VOLCANIC CORDILLERA

I HAD NEVER KNOWN THAT A VOLCANO COULD BREATHE.
Not a gentle inhalation, but a rhythmic panting, as if the mountain were gasping, short of breath. But from our vantage point on a ridge top just south of Arenal Volcano, the sound was unmistakable. Then suddenly, a burst of yellow smoke billowed into the sky, followed seconds later by the cracking thunder of another eruption.

Located in the north-central highlands of Costa Rica, Arenal is one of the most enthusiastically active volcanoes in the world. Since 1968, when it emerged from a long period of dormancy, it has been in a constant state of eruption, spewing ash and lava into the air every two or three hours, every day of the year.

Arenal is only one in a long skein of active volcanoes forming the mountainous spine of Central America, and the eastern boundary of the legendary Ring of Fire. Costa Rica alone has no fewer than two hundred volcanoes along its length, though most are no longer active, and are being slowly eroded away by wind and water. Yet there remain a handful—Poas, Irazu, Turrialba, Rincon de la Vieja, and, most dramatically, Arenal—to remind us that boiling magma still lies just below the surface.

Few places in the world have remained so consistently active for such a protracted period as Central America. There is evidence that volcanic activity in the region has continued virtually without pause since the time of the dinosaurs, some hundred million years ago. For most of that time, what is today Costa Rica was part of an oceanic arc of volcanic islands stretching between North and South America.

It was not until the late Pliocene, only three million years ago, that Costa Rica finally emerged completely from the sea, creating the slender isthmus that today links the two Americas. Four major mountain ranges, or *cordilleras*, have shaped the country along the oddly diagonal northwest-southeast trend it takes on the map today. In each of these ranges are mountains still on the rise, and volcanoes with fire still gnawing at their bellies. The restless shifting of crustal plates beneath the surface has never ceased.

There is something inexplicably addictive to volcano watching. I have spent many long, happy days content to simply sit, watch, and listen, and wait for the next explosion. But while daylight eruptions are impressive, the real fireworks begin at night. To sleep in Arenal's shadow is to know a humbling sense of vulnerability. Violent explosions shake you from your dreams and send you racing to the window. In the darkness an eruption creates dazzling fountains of incandescence, as molten rock shoots high into the sky, and tumbles back down in a cascade of sparks and fire.

To the people of modern Costa Rica, this volcanic heritage has been simultaneously a blessing and a curse. The Central Valley, where most Costa Ricans live, is lined with rich volcanic soils, a legacy of the volcanoes guarding its northern edge. While tropical soils are often shallow and short-lived, these highland valleys are lined with coffee and fruit.

At the same time, Costa Ricans have had to live with the earthquakes and eruptions such active regions produce. A catastrophic earthquake in 1991 tore apart much of the low-lying Caribbean coastline, destroying highways and bridges, while lifting navigable canals completely out of the water.

Typically, however, Costa Rica's volcanoes are not killers. Neither are they wholly benign—seventy-eight people in a nearby village died on a single day in 1968 when Arenal exploded without warning. Since that time, however, there have been few casualties, except for several would-be mountaineers struck down by flying rock or poisonous gases on misguided attempts to reach Arenal's barren

Left:

Eruptions are often accompanied by thundering explosions, and a plume of gray ash.

Opposite:

Fading dusk silhouettes Arenal's symmetrical cone.

summit. On the other active volcanoes, especially Poas and Irazu, periodic explosions of ash and smoke cause considerable anxiety, but little damage.

Major lava flows, like the molten rivers of Hawaii's Kiluaea, are rare among Costa Rica's volcanoes. Still, at Arenal, the lava occasionally pushes its way far enough downslope to encounter—and obliterate—living forest. Thirty years ago a massive flow on the mountain's southwest side buried everything in its path, while leaving trees untouched a few meters away.

I've walked along a lovely forest trail at Arenal that suddenly vanishes at the foot of what looks like nothing more than a massive slag heap. Climbing steeply up the cinders and rugged, black lava, I emerged at the top of a broad expanse of rock, raw and broken, the type of lava that geologists describe using a remarkable Hawaiian word: aa. In places, steam still rises from fissures in the rock, even after a generation.

It is an odd sight to stand on this lifeless wasteland, a stone's throw from the unbroken crown of a living forest—at eye level. And Arenal, meanwhile, looms above—an ominous puff of steam emerging from its summit.

With its sharp profile and explosive habits, Arenal is the wild child of Costa Rican volcanoes; most are far better behaved. Poas Volcano, fifty kilometers to the southeast of Arenal, could not be more dissimilar. Where Arenal is steep-sided and barren, Poas is massive and broad-shouldered, its slopes cloaked in dense forests. But most strikingly, while a climb to Arenal's summit is tantamount to suicide, thousands of people stream to the lip of Poas's crater every year.

The crater at Poas is a monumental sight, an enormous open boil on the earth's surface, almost two kilometers across and three hundred meters deep. Although Poas is classified as active, major eruptions are rare and not generally explosive; it seems to be content with the occasional burst of steam and gas. Most of this comes from a small lake, the color of pea soup, which bubbles like a witch's cauldron on the crater floor.

Poas has always had a special significance to the Costa Ricans, perhaps because its 2,708-meter summit so dominates the northern skyline of the Central Valley. A traditional pilgrimage march to the summit takes place every year on March 19, St. Peter's Day.

The mountain's status caused it to be declared a national protected area in 1939, long before the advent of the national park system. Unfortunately, this designation had no enforcement, and its forested slopes continued to be cleared for farms.

In 1970 it became one of the first components in Costa Rica's fledgling park system. Today, a quarter of a century later, it is the most popular park in the system for both foreign tourists and Costa Ricans alike—over 200,000 people visited Poas in 1993. In part, this popularity is due to its proximity to the Central Valley, an easy hour's drive from virtually anywhere, but Poas is also a crowd-pleaser—a drive-in park with a single awe-inspiring view.

At 2,708 meters high, this bulky mountain straddles the Continental Divide, gathering clouds around itself during the day, a typical phenomenon in tropical mountains. As a result, the crater is often lost to the mist by mid-morning. Late-rising visitors often arrive at Poas to see little more than a fog-bank, and stand shivering in the unexpected cold—another function of the high elevation.

Fortunately, there is much more to Poas than a single viewpoint. Because of its altitude, there is an extensive stand of elfin forest, dense tangles of trees and shrubs dwarfed by the persistent wind and chill. Trails cut into the forest resemble dark tunnels, filled with unfamiliar sounds.

There are a host of birds that specialize in these highland forests, most never seen at lower elevations. My favorite is a

drab little thing known as the slaty flow-erpiercer. The name of this peg-billed bird is well earned. It makes its way in the world by drinking nectar from flowers, not in the conventional, useful-to-the-plant way, but by picking a hole near the base of the flower and stealing it. If, however, a resident hummingbird catches one doing this, it will aggressively chase the thief off.

From the summit of Poas, the highlands drop sharply into the vast Caribbean Basin. Much of this slope is still cloaked in forest, which, because of the abundant rainfall, is laced with waterfalls. This is easily one of the loveliest parts of the country. But the forests soon give way to the first farms, and then, entering the hot, humid lowlands, to large-scale industrial plantations, especially of bananas.

Fortunately, an important section of the Caribbean slope of the Cordillera Central has been preserved within one of the largest national parks in Costa Rica: Braulio Carrillo. It is also one of the most surprising, a vast rainforest wilderness within a half-hour drive of San José. The park is named for an early-nineteenth-century president of the republic who, while considered something of a despot, worked hard to consolidate the young nation and to forge links across the rugged isthmus, connecting the two coasts.

The symbolism is appropriate, since the park itself grew out of a planned highway designed precisely with this in mind: to connect the Central Valley to the Caribbean. In 1973, when the new highway was proposed, the only access to the Caribbean lowlands was by means of several slow, narrow roads that meandered through the highlands.

The most logical route for the new highway led across a low pass in the Cordillera Central and down through this untouched forest wilderness. When an environmental impact study was commissioned, there was suddenly great concern

that the road would compromise, and even lead to the destruction of, the entire area. In response, the park service decided to protect the forest corridor through which the highway was built, and Braulio Carrillo Park was created in 1978.

Always outspoken, Alvaro Ugalde speaks frankly about the evolution of this magnificent park. "Braulio Carrillo grew out of the decision to build the road, not the other way around. Then we began to think about this area, which had never been considered for a park. But we wanted more than just a strip of park on either side of the road. Parks should be big and rounded, not like worms!"

For that reason, the park now includes several entire watersheds and a remarkable diversity of eco-systems from mountain tops to lowland forests.

Today, the drive from San José to Limón takes only a few hours, with cars and trucks rushing in either direction. I often wonder how drivers on that highway consider the landscape that they are speeding past. For myself, I can think of few highways in the world that traverse such irresistible terrain, a landscape virtually unchanged from before the arrival of Europeans.

Just a few steps off this highway lies a world few humans—perhaps no one—has ever traversed. Jaguars still haunt these isolated ridges and valleys, as do giant tapir and crested eagles, animals virtually extinct elsewhere in Central America.

You and I are not likely to see any of them, even in a lifetime of hiking in Braulio Carrillo; wild creatures are never easy to see in a tropical forest. If you are fortunate, you might spot a fresh tapir track in the mud after a brief rain shower, or see vultures overhead, a sure sign that a jaguar has abandoned the previous night's prey. Still, it does the heart good just to know they are there, that there remain places in which human affairs are secondary, where life can thrive without needing to know we even exist.

Although we may not see a jaguar or tapir, the forest is far from lifeless. In the cool of morning and evening, the trees are filled with the songs of birds, whistles and chirps both eloquent and jarring. There are people, of course, who can identify the source of every call—even without seeing the bird. But for most of us, it is enough simply to listen.

Yet there is one sound, common and distinct, that is recognizable to even the novice ear—and it is, happily, one of the most beautiful of tropical birds, the blue-crowned motmot. In the forests of Braulio Carrillo, the sound of a motmot is never far.

A motmot's call is like its name, a soft murmur of a sound, woop-oop, that carries a surprising distance through the forest. In places you may hear four or five of them at a time, as they announce their territory or try to lure a potential mate. But while hearing motmots is easy, finding them in the thick tangle of the understory is a decided challenge.

Motmots are intriguing in a variety of ways, not the least being the design of their tails. Of the half dozen species found in Costa Rica, all but one have what are known as racket tails: a pair of elongated tail feathers from which the barbs have been removed from a section near the end, leaving small paddles. No one has any real idea why they are there, but they are unique to motmots.

One clue is that motmots tend to sway their tails back and forth like a pendulum while sitting quietly at their perch, using the racket as a kind of semaphore. Some observers have suggested they do this when they are anxious, perhaps when a predator is close by. But if the birds are nervous about being eaten, one would think they would want to divert attention from themselves, not attract it by wagging their tail for all to see.

In addition, baby motmots have complete tails, and only in adulthood do rackets form. For many years, it was thought

Left, above:

The 'hotlips' flower is one of a number of rain forest plants used in traditional medicine.

below:

This tiny orchid, Encyclia radicans, grows directly on the ground at the edge of highland forests.

Opposite:

Impatiens form a brilliant carpet beneath La Paz Waterfall, a sacred place to many Costa Ricans.

that mature motmots plucked the feathers out of the tail to create their rackets, until someone noticed that the offending feathers are simply more loosely attached, and fall out naturally during the course of normal motmot behavior.

And finally, male and female motmots are essentially identical, so rackets do not seem to be some sort of showy breeding trait, like those of so many gaudily decorated species. So motmots remain happy enigmas, lovely and little understood, eating insects and butterflies, and twitching their gaudy tails.

Along the forests of the Cordillera, there is no distinct dry season; it is always soggy. Costa Rica's weather is essentially defined by two factors—prevailing winds and topography. Persistent trade winds from the Caribbean dump their moisture on the eastern slope of the Cordillera, making this one of the wettest regions of the country, with a mean annual rainfall in excess of five meters. (The highest rainfall, in the forests of Tapanti to the south, exceeds six meters; measurable rain fell on 359 days during 1968.)

On the mountains' western side, where most Costa Ricans live, the situation is dramatically different. Here there is a marked "rain shadow" effect; the high mountains of the Cordillera sweep the moisture out of the clouds, leaving little for the land to the west.

Lacking the four distinct seasons of temperate regions, Costa Ricans make do with just two. They refer to them simply as summer and winter. The dry season, generally between January and April, is "summer" (despite the awkward technicality that it occurs in the Northern Hemisphere's winter). The advent of the rains in May, on the other hand, begins the long Costa Rican "winter."

Nowhere in Costa Rica are the seasons more pronounced than in the country's northwest corner, on the slopes of the Cordillera de Tilarán. The rains are typically heavy along its eastern slope,

Opposite:

In Tapanti, one of the wet-
est corners of Costa Rica,
moss covers everything.

Right, clockwise:

Leaf-cutter ants demolish
an aroid flower; a daddy-
long-legs, or harvestman,
patrols a rain forest leaf;
waterdroplets decorate a
small leaf after a brief
shower, Monteverde
Cloud Forest; the huge
leaf of the 'poor-man's
umbrella', Irazu National
Park.

Overleaf:

A rufous-tailed jacamar
prepares to carry a small
insect back to its nest.

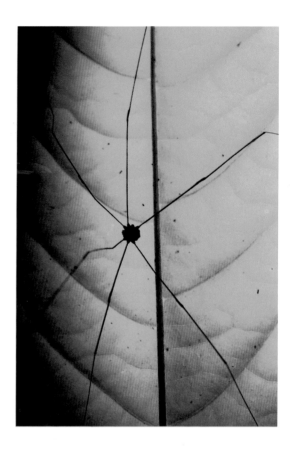

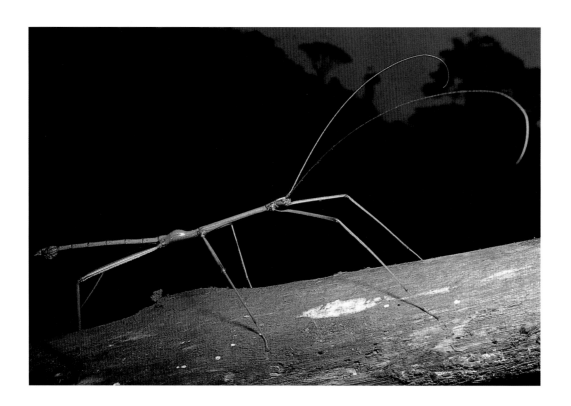

Left:

One of many species of stick-mimic insects in the forests of Braulio Carrillo

Opposite:

The deadly tropical wandering spider protects its egg case.

but to the west is the driest place in the country, the province of Guanacaste.

In the highlands of the Tilarán, the climate is cool and pleasant. For that reason, much of it has long been turned over to agriculture, to farms and pasture. Excellent dairy country, this is the source of most of the nation's cheese. And in the tiny settlement of Monteverde, a small group of expatriate North Americans created a modest private nature reserve that would one day become one of the most famous in the world: the Monteverde Cloud Forest.

Monteverde is not a national park, but a private reserve founded in 1972 by a small group of local farmers and biologists, in part to protect the watershed above the dairy farms. For many years now, the reserve has been owned and operated by the Centro Cientifico Tropical, a private organization that manages two other protected areas as well. Once it was established, the reserve quickly began to attract the attention of biologists and conservationists as a unique example of montane forest. In the intervening years, with the help of private donations from people all over the world, Monteverde has become the largest single private reserve in Costa Rica. And it is still growing, largely through the creation of the adjoining Bosque Eterno de los Niños: the Children's Eternal Forest. Begun as a fundraising drive for Monteverde among European schoolchildren, the Children's Forest now protects much of the threatened watershed on Monteverde's eastern slope.

The heart of the reserve straddles the Continental Divide, where clouds gather in a fairyland forest, eternally damp. It is a place of frogs and ferns, and a thousand kinds of fungus. It is also a muddy place, but this does not dissuade the thousands of people who flock to Monteverde from all parts of the globe every year. Nor does the abominable access road the locals seem resolute not to improve.

Meanwhile, Monteverde has become well known for a new, and far more ominous, reason. For while this reserve is protected, hopefully for all time, there are troubling signs which may have consequences far beyond its boundaries. Consider, for example, the golden toad.

Known only from Monteverde, in the spongy elfin forest atop the Continental Divide, the golden toad was discovered less than a generation ago. Every year when the first rains created pools on the forest floor, the male toads would gather and call, trying to attract a mate. Five years ago, the toads did not come to the pools, nor has a single toad been seen since then.

Is the golden toad extinct, and if so, from what cause? The forest itself seems unchanged, the climate consistent, the pools of water seemingly as they always have been. Nevertheless, something has happened to the toads. Perhaps, as has been proposed, frogs and toads are bellweathers of climatic change, or only the first of many organisms who may soon be affected by the diminished ozone layer. In this way, they may be like the canaries kept caged in the mineshaft to detect oxygen levels—if the canary dies, the story goes, the people are next.

It could be that some golden toads remain on some isolated ridge crest further along the Cordillera de Tilarán. Or they could be gone forever. The search for them goes on. Whatever the outcome, the missing toads provide new evidence that there is much we do not understand about nature and the often mysterious ways in which it functions.

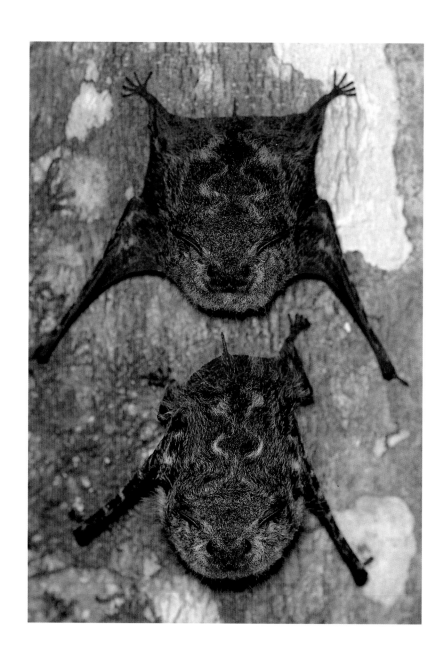

Left:

A pair of sac-winged bats
spend the day clinging to
a tree trunk.

Opposite:

Unlike its three-toed
cousin, the two-toed sloth
is active at night, with
thick fur to shed the rain
and the mountain cold.

THE UNTIRING SUN

THE DRY NORTHWEST

THE WATER IS BLACK AND TEPID, a perfect nursery for mosquitos. Where months ago clear water flowed, there are now no more than a few stagnant pools. It will be another month before the first rains bring the return of fresh water. For now, this murky puddle is probably the only standing water for miles in any direction. Gathered along its edge in the quiet of early evening is a band of coatis, drinking deeply.

Water is scarcely at a premium in most of Costa Rica. Because of the high mountains along its central spine, rivers and streams are never far away, carrying extravagant amounts of rainfall tumbling toward the sea. But in Santa Rosa National Park, along the northwestern coast, the annual dry season is predictable and profound. Virtually no rain falls between the months of December and May and, as a result, the many seasonal streams slow and finally vanish, leaving only a few scattered pools.

Living things are invariably tied to water, and in Santa Rosa, these fetid waterholes may be all that stand between life and death for the animals that live here. But waterholes are also dangerous places. Predators use them as well, lying in wait for the animals that must inevitably come to drink. For that reason, an animal at a waterhole is always wary.

Before they lower their heads to drink, the coatis scan nervously, listening and smelling the air around them. One older female stands guard on the bank, watching out for the band that is in her care. Assured that there is no danger, they finally begin to drink, their heads down and their tails held straight up—a row of furry flagpoles. Moments later, they scamper off into the safety of the thick brush.

As the sun climbs, it brings the first stinging heat of the day. Four collared peccaries emerge silently from the trees on tiny dancer's feet, drink quickly, and scutter off into the forest. Midday is quiet—and beastly hot. Mosquitos hum around our heads, but nothing comes to drink but a few timid doves.

Most of the animals that visit the waterhole are cautious, sensitive to danger. But not the little hermit. Brazenly, this tiny hummingbird comes to take its bath, looks at us, and buzzes straight over, hovering just inches from my face. Then, assured we mean no harm, it returns to hover over the pool, a foot above the water's surface. Suddenly, it drops down into the water with the tiniest splash, and then retreats to an overhanging twig to preen and dry. In a blink, it is gone.

Rainforest is easily seen in Costa Rica, but few people are prepared for the leafless, tinder-dry forests of Santa Rosa. Here, a palette of browns, golds, and ochres replaces the shades of green so typical elsewhere. Leaves crackle unexpectedly underfoot, and the air shimmers in the heat.

This is the tropical dry forest—an apparent oxymoron. While threatened tropical rainforest garners headlines, this arid counterpart remains one of the rarest natural ecosystems in Central America. Caught in the rain shadow of continuous mountains, dry forests once lined the Pacific coast from Mexico to central Costa Rica. Today less than 2 percent survives intact, and only a tiny fraction of that is protected within parks or reserves.

Dry forest has been decimated largely because it makes ideal cattle country—easily cleared, burned, and turned into pasture. At first glance, this part of Costa Rica more closely resembles the ranchland of Montana or Wyoming than it does the humid tropics. Over the past two hundred years, vast areas of forest have been cleared to make room for cattle. No place in Costa Rica, other than the densely populated Central Valley, has seen a heavier human hand.

Today, the largest extant dry forest in all of Mesoamerica is within Santa Rosa National Park. There is some irony in this fact, since it was not this threatened

Preceding pages:

The Tempisque River wanders through the arid forests of Palo Verde National Park.

Opposite:

A migrant willet, escaping the North American winter, feeds at sunset along a Santa Rosa beach.

Overleaf:

Huge flocks of waterfowl gather in the shallow pools of Palo Verde.

forest that helped push Santa Rosa toward protection, but a nineteenth-century battle fought over its arid soil. The Battle of Santa Rosa, in March of 1856, was one of the pivotal events in Costa Rica's bid for nationhood. It was here that a volunteer army of nine thousand Costa Ricans beat back an invasion from Nicaragua, led by U.S.-born William Walker and a private army of mercenaries. Walker had hopes of conquering all of the isthmus and creating a personal empire, but he got no farther south than Santa Rosa.

The event is one of the most celebrated in the nation's history. Imagine, then, how Costa Ricans reacted when, in the 1930s, the entire area was bought by Anastasio Somoza, dictator of Nicaragua. That this historic spot could be owned by a foreigner—and Somoza was considered particularly loathesome—was unthinkable.

It was not until 1966 that the Costa Rican government was able to buy the land back from Nicaragua, and made plans to turn it into a national historical monument. When a team of biologists was asked by the government to evaluate the area for park status, they quickly realized what a treasure it was. Here were large tracts of intact forest, filled with wildlife, and long, untouched beaches where sea turtles gathered every year to nest. So in 1971, a ten-thousand-hectare parcel of land between the Panamerican Highway and the ocean became a national park. A period ranchhouse, or *casona*, still stands near the battle site, the historical centerpiece for the park.

The first administrator at Santa Rosa was the young Alvaro Ugalde, fresh out of college, with no experience whatsoever in park management. "When I first went to Santa Rosa twenty-five years ago, I thought ten thousand hectares was the biggest ecosystem on earth! And then, of course, you find out this is a very tiny piece of land and that there is very little of this ecosystem protected anywhere else." In time, new parcels of land would be

Left:
Wood storks roost in large numbers on islands in the Tempisque River.

Opposite, above:
Only a handful of jabiru storks survive in all of Central America; Palo Verde is one of their last nesting sites.
below:
A roseate spoonbill flies off in search of a feeding pond.

added, until today Santa Rosa is almost four times as big as it was in that first year.

Typically, however, there was much more to creating a national park than simply signing the papers. "There were squatters all over the place," remembers Ugalde, "and they were starting to cut down the forest. One of the neighboring landowners had even stolen part of the park land by moving his fence inside." Mario Boza and Ugalde would work tirelessly for months to publicize what was going on, trying to spur the government into taking action. Finally, the money was allocated to move the squatters to land outside the park boundaries. For the first time, a portion of tropical dry forest had been set aside not for the production of cattle, but for the conservation of a unique ecosystem that had nearly disappeared.

The adaptations of plants to a prolonged annual drought are as ingenious as any in the rain forest. Like many of the trees in Santa Rosa, the gumbo limbo drops its leaves during the dry season to prevent the loss of precious moisture. But the gumbo limbo also has another, more sophisticated, trick. Its distinctive peeling red bark (the source of a popular nickname, "the tourist tree") reveals a green inner skin. The green, of course, is from chlorophyll, contained within the cells of the young bark. The chlorophyll allows the tree to continue photosynthesizing while its leafless neighbors must wait until the first rains.

In the drier parts of the park, particularly along the rocky coastline, grow tall columnar cactus, sometimes in the open, at other times below the trees of the forest. These forest cactus, too, play a subtle game. When there are leaves on the trees, the cactus is shaded and goes hungry. But when the dry season comes and the trees lose their leaves, the cactus is exposed to the sun and begins to feed hungrily on the light.

One of the most striking trees in Santa Rosa is the guanacaste, from which

the province derives its name; it is also the national tree of Costa Rica. Typically massive with a spreading canopy, it is reminiscent of the graceful acacias of the African savannah. But its handsome form is an artifact of deforestation—in a natural forest, the guanacaste would be crowded by other trees, making it grow narrower and more confined.

The guanacaste is sometimes referred to as the ear tree, a reference to its oddly curled seed pod. Thousands of these seeds are dropped by the trees every year, yet although the seeds are abundant, the trees are not. One explanation for this, proposed by biologist Daniel Janzen, weaves an intriguing story of evolutionary time-travel.

Janzen noticed that when guanacaste seeds fall into pastures they are eagerly eaten by cattle and horses, and only then do they take root and grow. "These hard, dormant seeds do not germinate unless the seed coat has been scarified by wear, gut passage, or mechanical filing," Janzen explains. But how did the trees disperse their seeds before there were cattle? Janzen theorizes that the answer may reach all the way back to the Pleistocene, when large herbivores—including a ground sloth the size of a grizzly bear—roamed these forests. Perhaps they consumed the vast quantities of fallen guanacaste seeds, and spread the tree throughout the region. Not all biologists accept this notion (untestable hypotheses being somewhat unpopular in the scientific community), but it is an intriguing theory.

Today, the seeds of the guanacaste are often eaten by yellow-naped parrots, but with their strong beaks, they break open the seed itself, doing little for the next generation of guanacaste trees. Parrots and parakeets are among the most conspicuous creatures at Santa Rosa. For unlike terrestrial animals, which must travel through the forest silently to avoid detection, parrots fly everywhere at full volume with a loud, grating scream.

Apparently, they have little to fear in the air, but they are invariably quiet when they land, because they are more vulnerable.

If you have ever wondered why parrots are green, you haven't tried to look for them in a tree. Most also have brilliant red and yellow plumage, but show them only on the wing. When they land, the color is hidden, and they vanish instantly into the foliage.

Yellow-naped parrots were once common throughout most of Costa Rica's Pacific slope, but as the forest disappeared, so did they. Like all parrots, they need dead, standing trees—common to mature forests—in which to nest. Young second-growth forest has little standing deadwood, and therefore few parrots. Even worse, however, have been the depredations of the pet trade, for yellow-napes are among the world's best talkers, and few birds are more prized as caged pets. For them, these protected forests are a final refuge.

While this species hangs on, others have not been so lucky. The scarlet macaw, largest and most spectacular of all Costa Rican parrots, has vanished from the forests of Santa Rosa. For the macaw, protection came too late. Today there may be less than a few hundred of these birds left anywhere in the country; there are probably more in captivity in hotel lobbies and private homes than remain in the wild.

Although the scarlet macaw is gone, several other species on the brink of extinction have persisted at Santa Rosa— tapir, spider monkey, and the yellow-naped parrot. All three serve as a living measure of a healthy forest, and are only found where large tracts of forest remains.

Two other monkey species, the howler and the capuchin, also thrive in Santa Rosa. The two could not be more different. Howlers are leaf eaters and as a result gain little energy from their food. They are sluggish and largely sedentary, sitting so quietly in the trees that you can often pass directly underneath them and

Left:

Fallen leaves on the forest floor, Santa Rosa National Park.

Opposite:

With astonishing accuracy, a katydid mimics a dried leaf.

Overleaf:

Lingering clouds on the summit of the Guanacaste range bring no moisture to the arid northwest.

never see their watchful eyes. Capuchins, on the other hand, are gregarious and eternally curious. Omnivores, they seem to be always on patrol, looking for food, and getting it wherever they can.

We tend to think of monkeys as contented, good-natured animals, living in the treetops on a diet of fruits and berries. It has only been in recent years that we have learned more disturbing things about our smaller cousins. During the course of Jane Goodall's pioneering work with chimpanzees, she recounts discovering, to her horror, that they were capable of deliberate, calculated murder and infanticide. Intelligence, it seems, comes at a cost.

A group of Austrian biologists recently told me an electrifying story about a troop of capuchins they had been studying in the forest at Santa Rosa. One afternoon, they sat watching them leisurely eating their way through the canopy when, suddenly, the monkeys' mood changed and they became instantly alert.

Ahead, in the trees, sat a group of squirrels feeding on nuts. At first it seemed the monkeys had thoughts of chasing the squirrels away from an easy food source, or perhaps simply stealing it from them—but it quickly became obvious that the squirrels themselves were the target.

Working as a team, the monkeys fanned out through the branches and, one after another, cornered, caught, and killed the squirrels. For the next hour, the biologists watched as the monkeys sat in the treetops and devoured their prey.

Such sights are rare in the tropical forest. The life and death dramas such as one sees every day on the African plains occur here as well, but are hidden from view. No more than a handful of people have ever seen a jaguar make a kill, or a harpy eagle snatch a monkey from the treetops. But they occur just as normally as a snake eating a frog.

At the western edge of Santa Rosa National Park, a rocky escarpment drops sharply to the sea. Here the forest gives way

Left:

Beneath the peeling bark of the gumbo limbo tree is the green photosynthetic skin that sustains it when its leaves are gone.

Opposite:

The sere landscape of Santa Rosa National Park at the height of the dry season.

Left:

Never relaxed on the
ground, a white-faced
capuchin climbs to the
safety of a roadside tree.

Opposite:

The largest of the new
world primates:
the spider monkey.

to mangrove estuaries and broad expanses of sandy beach. It is a popular place for surfers, who negotiate a ghastly rock-filled road down the escarpment for a chance to work the long-breaking Pacific rollers.

These beaches seem otherworldly, backed by forest, untouched by human activity: a beach without hotels is becoming an increasingly rare sight. Outside the park, beaches that a decade ago were on the edge of wilderness are quickly being snatched up by developers; soon those at Santa Rosa and the other coastal national parks may be the only ones left without hotels and resorts.

This would be reason enough to be grateful for the beaches of Santa Rosa. But there is also another, more compelling reason for their protection—these are among the last vital nesting beaches for sea turtles. On Nancite Beach, only a kilometer long, occurs one of the greatest natural gatherings on earth: the *arribada* (arrival) of the olive ridley. At one time ridleys nested on beaches all along the Pacific coast of Mesoamerica; today only a handful of untouched beaches remain where they can lay their eggs in safety and where they are protected from poachers.

Every year, responding to signals that we cannot understand, these turtles come ashore en masse at tiny Nancite, as many as forty-five thousand in a night. During these enormous, chaotic assaults on the beach, turtles scramble over one another in their frenzy to nest, and often uncover the eggs of other turtles in the rush to lay their own.

These massive *arribadas*, known only among ridley turtles, are like the schooling of fish; biologists refer to it as "swamping" the predators. The more turtles that nest at one time, the more likely that someone else's eggs will be found and eaten by the host of predators that wait to do just that. But things at Nancite are not quite so clear-cut.

As many as half of the million eggs laid on Nancite during an *arribada* will never hatch, not because of predation,

but because the Nancite turtles possess a significantly lower reproductive rate than turtles elsewhere. The reasons for this are still unknown, but because the numbers of mature ridley turtles that return every year remains relatively stable, this unexpected egg mortality does not seem to have a serious impact on the survival of the species. Nor does the low survival rate of young turtle hatchlings: Only a tiny percentage of turtles that emerge from the sand and head toward the surf survive to be nesting adults. (Some details of this ordeal are described in Chapter Four.)

Four out of the seven species of sea turtles in the world today nest on Costa Rican beaches. Besides the ridley, there is the green, the hawksbill, and the leatherback. All are considered endangered, for despite the fact that their breeding beaches are protected in Costa Rica, there are simply too few of them to be invulnerable to an oil spill or other environmental catastrophe. If tiny Nancite beach were destroyed, the ridley turtle would likely go with it, and a lineage that began two hundred and fifty million years ago could end.

Sixteen kilometers inland from the sea, the coastal plain begins to rise abruptly toward the eroded remnants of two volcanoes, Orosi and Cacao. Their combined massif forms the northern end of the Cordillera de Guanacaste; from here the land drops away to the Nicaraguan border and the enormous inland sea of Lake Nicaragua.

Nearly twenty years after Santa Rosa became a national park, a new park was created that would connect it to the mountains and, in the process, attempt to enclose an entire ecosystem. "Guanacaste National Park was created," explained Mario Boza, "after Daniel Janzen's research indicated that many species travel between the lowlands and the volcanos every year. In the dry season, for instance, there is still a lot of humidity and cloudiness in the highlands, which

Left:

Wearily dragging herself
from the sea, an olive
ridley comes ashore to lay
her eggs.

Opposite:

On isolated Nancite Beach,
thousands of turtles may
come ashore en masse to
nest.

attracts a lot of species."

Insects, birds, and even perhaps some mammals make these seasonal migrations up and down the Pacific slope. Without a forest corridor, such a journey would eventually be impossible.

The Costa Rican government supported the idea for a park, but had no money to finance it. Instead Janzen himself, exchanging his field clothes for a suit and tie, spent several years fundraising in the United States. His success was legendary, for he raised millions of dollars, endowing the new park with funds for land acquisition, management, and biological research.

Janzen's success seems even more remarkable when one considers that the new park was little more than a motley collection of farms, open pasture, and scattered trees. This is quite literally a park for the future: one day, it is hoped, natural regeneration will bring back the closed-canopy forest that once covered the entire region. For that to happen, the many small patches of native forest dotting the landscape must expand, serving as genetic reservoirs from which species can spread and thrive.

The biggest enemy of regeneration is fire. Fire is a natural component of a dry forest; however, the exotic grasses, brought in for cattle, that now cover much of the region burn too fast and too hot, overwhelming the young native trees struggling to gain a foothold. As a result, the grasslands persist and the forest cannot expand. Fighting fires has become a major responsibility for the park staff. On occasion all hands are called in, from researchers to cooks and mechanics.

Meanwhile, seventy-five kilometers to the south of Santa Rosa, fire is less an issue at Palo Verde National Park. Still technically part of the dry-forest ecosystem, Palo Verde is otherwise strikingly dissimilar. Located on the floodplain of the Tempisque River, it is flat country, dotted with sharp limestone outcrops, the remains of ancient coral reefs. Every year,

as the heavy rains come, the rocky, impermeable soil becomes saturated, creating fertile pools and lagoons. These, in turn, form the single most important gathering place for waterfowl in Central America. Huge numbers of ducks, ibis, storks, and other waterbirds converge on these flooded fields; some are tropical residents, but others are migrants, escaping the northern winter.

Palo Verde is not a showy place; there is none of the physical drama of Poas Volcano, or the romantic lushness of Manuel Antonio. It is a park less because of its scenery than for the benefit of the wildlife that depends upon it. And the abundance of living things at Palo Verde is prodigious indeed.

In every ditch and backwater, great egrets and tiger-herons patrol for small fish, while kingfishers perch on trees and telephone lines, scanning the water below. Flocks of black-bellied whistling ducks darken the shallower grass-filled fields. And on islands in the Tempisque, wood storks and roseate spoonbills gather in enormous rookeries, blinding in the midday sun from the thick coating of whitewash.

Many of the birds of Palo Verde time their breeding to coincide with the early part of the dry season, for as the wet season's pools begin to contract in the heat, the small fish that will be food for young birds are concentrated within them. If the birds nest too late, the pools dry completely, the fish die, and the chicks starve.

By late April, Palo Verde is dry again, and the birds have dispersed. Some, like the whistling ducks, have begun their long journey north to Texas where they will nest. Others, like the spoonbills, will spread out over the coastal wetlands of Costa Rica and Nicaragua.

In May the skies darken and the rains begin in earnest, turning the dry forest green as trees quickly burst into leaf. Muddy waterholes fill and become rivers again, and the animals once more disperse into the forest in their never-ending search for food.

Collared peccaries are cautious as they approac a waterhole; they know predators often lie in wa nearby.

Superficially, the jaguarundi more closely resembles a weasel than a cat. Like most forest cats, they are shy and rarely seen.

EYES IN THE WATER

THE CARIBBEAN COAST

AT NIGHT, THE FOREST IS FILLED with eyes. From a dugout canoe, slipping quietly through the narrow waterways of Tortuguero National Park, a hand-held lamp reveals a world hidden by day. Caught by the light, pairs of orange eyes line the streams and canals; these are caiman, smaller cousins of the crocodile, out on their nocturnal prowl. In the branches overhead, twin discs of amber reveal a roving kinkajou. And everywhere, on the trunks of trees and along the water's edge, the light finds thousands of tiny emeralds—the twinkling eyes of hunting spiders.

Most of Costa Rica's Caribbean coast is as flat and featureless as the Pacific is rugged and dramatic. Except for a single isolated hill—the remnant core of an ancient volcano—there is nothing higher than three meters above sea level for more than a hundred kilometers along this coastline. A third of this is contained within Tortuguero Park. Low-lying and sodden, with some of the heaviest rainfall in the country, it is a labyrinth of rivers and *caños*—narrow streams, choked by vegetation. There are few trails on land, and these are often muddy and mosquito infested; it is an environment best traversed by boat.

From the water, the forest is a wall of green. Rivers form gaps in the forest, filled with light, in which the vegetation thrives from the top of the canopy to the ground in an unbroken curtain. Pass through and you step into darkness, even in midday. High above, on trees fifty meters high, sloths hang motionless in the breeze, while at the water's edge, tiny green herons stand in the shadows, staring into the water, waiting for a careless fish to rise. A few meters ahead, what looks like a stick suddenly breaks the water's surface, a wriggling fish impaled on it. It is not a stick, but an anhinga, a sharp-billed bird more at home underwater than in the air.

After the sun goes down, the forest comes alive. Most rainforest animals are active at night, not during the day; the darkness makes it easier to hide from both prey and predator, and offers welcome relief from the heat. Yet despite the increased activity, the forest is deceptively quiet. It is the silence of terror and stealth. Although the forest holds few dangers for humans, sudden death is an ever-present danger for other animals in the darkness; very few die of old age. Insects are snatched silently from the leaves by patrolling lizards. An arboreal snake stumbles onto a sleeping bird—and quickly seizes it. A puma bounds onto the back of a passing brocket deer, whose cries are silenced by the cat's powerful jaws.

As dawn approaches, most large animals search out dark holes or hollow logs, safe places in which to sleep away the day. In the rivers, caimans lose themselves among the dense tangles of floating branches along the shore. Insects often rely on camouflage—many are ingeniously veined and shaped to look like leaves—to simply blend into the background and wait for nightfall.

Even the gaudiest of creatures can sometimes hide in plain view. The red-eyed tree frog, one of the most colorful of rainforest animals, simply tucks his blue legs underneath his body and closes his bright red eyes, until all that's visible is his green skin. But even this is not enough. As the frog's skin dries, it pales, leaving just a whitish blotch on a leaf—designed to look like nothing more than a smear of bird droppings.

The luxuriant forests and narrow waterways of Tortuguero make up the last lowland wilderness on Costa Rica's Caribbean coast. In the last few decades almost all of the flat country between the Cordillera and the coast has been given over to agriculture, including massive banana plantations. As was the case with so many of the parks, Tortuguero was saved just in time. But it was not just the forests that first drew the park service's attention to the Tortuguero area, it was

Left:
Tree frogs climb with the use of large finger pads that serve as suction cups.

Opposite, clockwise:
With the first rains in May, hundreds of red-eyed tree frogs gather, looking for mates; two male frogs wrestle with one another over the attentions of a female; in copulation, the disparity in size is obvious: the female is much larger than the male.

sea turtles. In 1955 American biologist Archie Carr came to Tortuguero to study green turtles, which nest here every year in enormous numbers. Carr returned to the beaches at Tortuguero every season, raised his children among the canals and forested streams, and banded adult turtles as they came ashore to nest.

Since that time tens of thousands of nesting turtles have been tagged at Tortuguero, revealing much of what we know about their lives and travels. At the same time, several generations of young biologists both American and Costa Rican, have been introduced to the rigors and joys of field research. Among these were Mario Boza and Alvaro Ugalde, who in 1968 made a trip together to Tortuguero.

Along with them on that trip was then-president José Figueres, one of the most popular presidents in Costa Rican history, and his wife, Karen. In the ensuing years, Don José and Karen would become very important supporters of the national park system. Figueres's third term, 1970–74, is considered the golden age of Costa Rican parks because many of today's premier parks were created during that period—Poas, Santa Rosa, Manuel Antonio, and Tortuguero.

In the years that Carr worked at Tortuguero, he watched the nesting beaches increasingly fall prey to egg collectors and turtle hunters, and the numbers of returning turtles plummet. The turtles were protected by law on these nesting beaches, but there was little enforcement, and turtle hunting had a long history along this coast. As a result of the notion that turtle eggs have aphrodisiacal properties—there is enormous potential for profit in such things—millions of young turtles were doomed.

It has never been hard to decimate a turtle colony. Turtles invariably return to nest on the same beach where they were born, and once on shore, they are easy targets. When regulations forbid taking turtles on the beach, turtle hunters simply wait offshore in small boats; the turtles are sure to come.

Nothing, meanwhile, could be easier than collecting turtle eggs; one needs only to sit and wait for a female to come ashore and begin laying—and simply let the eggs drop into your hand. Or, if you'd prefer to sleep through the night, a trained eye can easily see the smooth patch of sand that indicates the futile efforts of a female turtle to hide her nest.

The creation of Tortuguero National Park in 1970 gave new hope for the turtles, and with the addition of guard patrols on the beach, the muscle to enforce the rules. (Ironically, *tortuguero* means "turtle hunter" as well as "a bunch of turtles.") Still, the problems did not disappear overnight. On my first trip to Tortuguero I saw men selling turtle meat and eggs openly on the streets of Limón. Although selling turtle meat is allowed by the government, the poaching of eggs still continues. But recently, turtle hunters have become turtle guides in what has now become a major industry at Tortuguero: tourism. There is added incentive now to protect the turtles, as there is potentially more money to be made by showing live turtles to foreigners than by trying to sell dead turtles on the black market.

In 1975 the park was expanded to include a large tract of inland forest, while to the north, the adjoining Barra del Colorado Wildlife Refuge added much more. Together the two parklands comprise over one hundred thousand hectares of land—a thousand square kilometers of beach, swamp, and primary forest.

The coast itself, broken only by the occasional debris-strewn river mouth, is a straight, monotonous beach of gray sand. In the heat of the day, that beach is unspeakably hot, and the surface of the sand often climbs above 45 degrees Celsius. The sun is direct and brutal, the only relief a humid breeze off the ocean.

The wing spots of the leaf-like automeris moth resemble huge eyes designed to startle predators.

Clockwise from upper left:
The hairy cup fungus is a common woodland species; morning glory flowers riefly on Cahuita's hot nds; Encyclia fragrans, sweet-smelling orchid, is und in lowland forests; graceful asymmetry haracterizes the forest eliconia.

verleaf:
ortuguero is an environ-ent dominated by water. owhere more than a eter above the sea level, e land is often inundat-d by torrential rains.

Several feet under the sand, still cool and moist, a jumble of young sea turtles is beginning its climb to the surface. Scrambling madly at the sand over their heads, they dig through the roof of their nest chamber, the loose sand trickling down between them and gradually raising the floor underneath. In time the first young turtle breaks through to the surface. What he finds there may mean the difference between life and death.

Hatching sea turtles time their emergence by the temperature of the sand. As the temperature begins to drop it is a sign of approaching dusk above. With luck they will come to the surface after dark, and close to the high tide, so that their race to the sea will be brief and shielded by darkness.

Occasionally, though, they are fooled by thick clouds, or take so long to emerge that the dawn catches them. In this case the odds, never favorable, are stacked decidedly against them, for the sun is deadly to a young turtle. Not only does daylight make a turtle more visible to predators, the heat may sap its strength even before it is free of the nest. It may simply perish there, having only poked its head out from beneath the sand. Nevertheless, once they have reached the surface, they cannot go back into the sand to wait for a better opportunity. They must move quickly.

If the new hatchling can somehow muster the strength and will to dig free, it will follow a powerful instinct and scramble madly toward the water. Crossing the open sand will be the most perilous few minutes in the turtle's life. A host of enemies is waiting—black vultures, coatis, coyotes, even ghost crabs appear out of nowhere when the turtle hatch is on, and gorge themselves on any young turtles unlucky enough to emerge in daylight. But that's not all. Logs and debris—even human footprints, too deep to escape— can also bar the way, and many turtles perish only meters from the surf.

When the first baby turtle reaches the water, it is often swept back up the beach by the surge, tumbling head over heels. Flippers still waving, it quickly comes upright, and turns again toward the water. Finally, the turtle is lifted from the sand by a wave and is carried down toward the sea; in a moment, its tiny head breaks the surface for its first breath of air.

Sadly, even here, the danger isn't over. I have watched a hatchling negotiate a hundred meters of scalding beach, only to be snatched out of the water at its moment of triumph by a frigatebird, hovering inches over the waves. Soaring upward in a swift arc, the frigate stalled in midair and tossed the young turtle back into its throat, swallowing it whole. Thus ended the short and arduous life of a baby green turtle.

Sharks, too, wait just beyond the surfline, and the water often boils as they feed on madly scattering hatchlings. No wonder, then, that only a tiny fraction of all the young turtles born on the beaches of Tortuguero will ever return to nest. Fortunately, enough turtles emerge at night, or when the tide is high, to successfully run the gauntlet on their sprint toward life.

For the adults who came ashore six weeks before, the journey was much less dangerous. Few predators will take on an adult sea turtle; their chief threat has always been human. Though their task is not dangerous, it requires enormous effort. Their weight supported by the water, sea turtles are wonderfully buoyant and graceful, but on land they are woefully heavy. Their urge to nest must be powerful, indeed, to get them to drag themselves from the water and up the sand. It is a natural drama that has been acted out on these sands since the days of the dinosaurs.

The nesting process is slow, laborious, and fascinating to watch. So intense is their effort and concentration that once they have begun laying the hundred or so

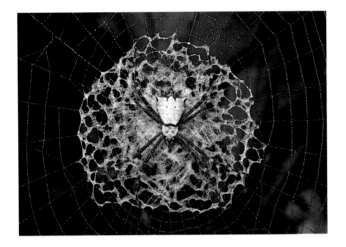

eggs—looking like so many ping-pong balls—they enter a kind of trance. Nothing on earth could stop them. At other times, though, they are more vulnerable. Bright lights can scare a turtle off the beach just as it is coming ashore, making it abandon the nesting effort. For that reason, flashlights and flash cameras are forbidden on the beach during the nesting season. Instead, guides take tourists stumbling in the dark, their dim lights covered with red filters designed to avoid disturbing the turtles just emerging from the surf.

By the time the sun rises, the nesting is done, and the females have returned to the sea. The only evidence of their passing are the semicircular "tread-marks" that mark their paths to and from the water. After a busy night, there may be dozens of these up and down the beach.

As the turtle's long night is ending, the day is just beginning in the nearby forest. Howler monkeys are the first to greet the dawn, and start their monstrous roaring even before the first color glows on the eastern horizon. By five o'clock the sun has still not appeared, but the sky is already light and flocks of parrots have begun their day, flying out over the canopy, their screeching unbridled. Meanwhile, in the forest below, the light grows slowly, and the air is still cool. This is the best time to go for a walk.

Many newcomers to the tropical forest enter with great anxiety, imagining it to be a hostile place, filled with danger and discomfort. Nothing looms larger in the pantheon of imagined horrors than poisonous snakes. A great deal is made of snakes, much of it irrational. Yet the fear of snakes is persistent and powerful, perhaps (as some have suggested) a genetic throwback to our days on the African savannah.

The fact is that seeing a snake is a rare event in the tropical forest. In hundreds of walks in the forests of Costa Rica I have only seen a handful of them, and only a fraction of those were actually venomous. And, without exception, every

Left, above:

Morning dew covers a spider's web with diamonds.

below:

The morpho butterfly is the most stunning in the tropical forests.

Opposite:

A leaf-mimic praying mantis is among the fiercest of insect predators; it will even attack a curious human.

snake that I've seen saw me first—and promptly headed south.

People are bitten by poisonous snakes in Costa Rica every year, but the vast majority of these are farmers and plantation workers who encounter snakes while they work in fields and orchards. Fortunately, few die from their bites, partially because snakes use their venom sparingly in their own defense, but also because every community hospital in Costa Rica has a good supply of antivenins.

One of the most legendary of Costa Rica's venomous snakes, and one of the most beautiful, is the fer-de-lance. The name is French, meaning "iron of the lance," a reference to its pointed head. It is said to be aggressive, although most things are bad-tempered when stepped on, the way most bites occur. But the fer-de-lance's fearsome reputation lives on, to the point that it is normally killed on sight. Unfortunately, few people are trained herpetologists, and there are many other snakes in the forest that resemble the fer-de-lance, many nonvenomous, and they too are often promptly dispatched—just to be on the safe side.

The sun rises quickly in the tropics; it seems nearly overhead by eight in the morning. This is the time to retreat from the heat and lay low, for during the long, torpid hours of midday, there is little movement in the forest. Even diurnal, or daytime-active, animals like monkeys pass the heat of the day stretched out on branches high in the trees, keeping activity to a minimum and trying to catch any slight breeze.

One animal, however, remains conspicuously active—the poison dart frog. No larger than your little fingernail, but a bright cherry red, this little frog is a colorful anomaly in a place where most things are cryptic and hidden. It is a classic example of aposematic coloration—if you are bad to eat, let everybody know it.

These frogs, and the dozens of other related species, each with a different

pattern of brilliant colors, carry potent toxins in their skins, long used by native peoples to tip their blow darts. These poisons would be lethal to any animal that ate the frog—but by that time it would already be too late for the frog. For that reason, the bright colors are thought to advertise the fact that the frog is toxic, heading off an attack while it is still early enough to do the frog some good.

Poison dart frogs spend most of their lives hopping about the forest floor, eating ants and termites (of which there is no shortage), but they begin their lives high in the canopy. Just after it has hatched on the ground, a young frog is carried up a nearby tree on its parent's back, and deposited in the natural pools of water that form in the rosettes of bromeliad plants. These pools are often filled with organic material and insect larvae, a rich source of food for the developing tadpole, and the spiny plant makes a good safe place to live. To make sure that the young frog has enough to eat, his mother returns several times in the weeks ahead and lays additional eggs. These will never hatch—they are infertile—but are designed to provide extra food for the young frog.

Much of what we know about these frogs, and about tropical ecosystems in general, has come through studies carried out over the last few decades at a handful of tropical research stations. One of the most legendary of these is La Selva, a private reserve on the western edge of the Caribbean lowlands. La Selva is owned by the Organization of Tropical Studies (OTS), a consortium of universities in the United States and Costa Rica, and serves as one of the world's foremost tropical teaching and research facilities.

The core area of primary forest at the La Selva reserve was owned by forester Leslie Holdridge, best known for his development of a classification system for tropical forests. Holdridge sold the land to OTS in 1968, and since that time the

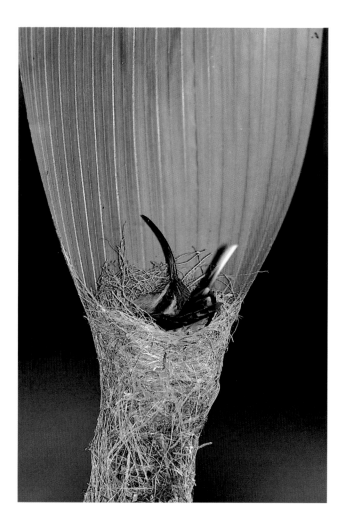

119

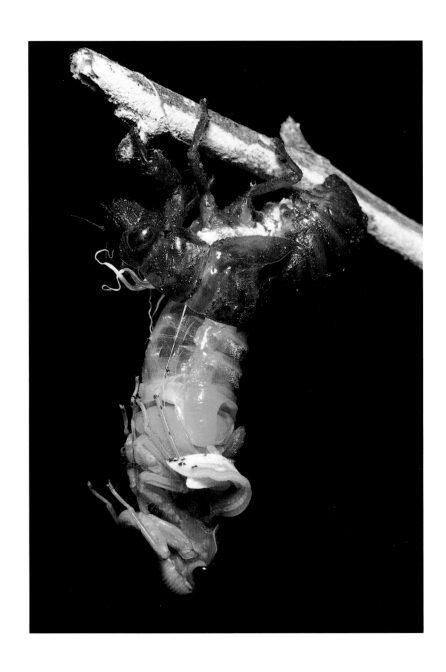

Left:

Under the protection of
darkness, a cicada is less
vulnerable as it emerges
from its old skin.

Opposite:

Using their large
mandibles, leaf-cutter
ants cut graceful arcs in
fresh green leaves.

reserve has grown to include a large tract of adjacent secondary forest and agricultural land.

La Selva is typically a beehive of scientific activity. At any one time, there may be a large group of international students studying tropical forest ecology and researchers from universities around the world studying subjects as diverse as termite behavior and tentmaking in bats. The forest is riddled with trails, laid out to provide access to almost every corner of the reserve. In places, these trails are paved, so that scientists working in the farthest reaches of the property can get there by bicycle. I recently saw a hummingbird sitting on its nest, casually watching as dozens of scientists whisked back and forth along a paved trail just below.

There are many private reserves in Costa Rica, some set aside for research purposes, like La Selva, while others encourage tourism, and use the income to enlarge their reserve. This makes them excellent neighbors to the national parks, for they enlarge the scope of the protected areas. In 1986, for example, Braulio Carrillo National Park was enlarged to connect with La Selva, creating a complete transect of forest from the top of the volcanoes to the Caribbean lowlands. In addition, two other private reserves exist alongside this La Selva/Braulio Carrillo corridor—Rara Avis and Selva Verde. Both are profit-making operations for their owners, yet by setting aside land for preservation rather than extraction, they help save the land and wildlife, again adding to the size and value of existing reserves. These intact forests have the potential to be more profitable, and more renewable, than forests cleared for agriculture or pastureland.

The southern Caribbean coast, south from Tortuguero, gradually becomes more ragged and broken. Several rocky headlands jut out from the coast on which fringing coral reefs have developed. Although they are modest by Caribbean

standards, there are the only such reefs along Costa Rica's eastern shore, the largest of which are contained within Cahuita National Park, created in 1970.

Unfortunately, the reefs at Cahuita have been severely damaged in the past two decades, partially from natural causes, but also by human activity. Hurricanes, to which this coast is prone, have repeatedly hammered the reef, breaking off large sections of coral. In addition, sediment carried down nearby rivers from deforested areas inland effectively smothers the living polyps. Compounding the problem have been the vast banana plantations all along this coast, which contribute chemical pollutants that may kill coral or stimulate the growth of algae which can blanket the reef

Already damaged, the reef at Cahuita was dealt a catastrophic blow in April 1991, when a 7.1 earthquake lifted entire sections of it above the waterline, killing what living coral remained. Elsewhere along the coast, the earthquake had similarly catastrophic effects. In less than a minute, highway bridges were destroyed and houses flattened, navigable canals were lifted dry, and rivers forced into new channels.

Although the coral reefs at Cahuita are not what they once were, there is still living coral in places farther south along the coast. And there remains much to see at Cahuita behind the beach. Besides the offshore reef, the park also protects a large patch of swamp forest, now one of the last pieces of coastal forest left in an area where beachside development is growing quickly.

It's a shame that few people walk the trails of Cahuita National Park. The climbing vines of vanilla orchids grow all along the trail, and the many open-limbed Cecropia trees harbor three-toed sloths; it is not uncommon to see half a dozen in a single morning's walk.

One of the most common animals throughout the park is the basilisk lizard.

A beach at Cahuita National Park.

A clutch of green turtle hatchlings emerges at the surface along the Tortuguero beach. Released from the sand, they must begin the perilous journey down to the water's edge.

To see an adult basilisk with its magnificent crest and finned back is to glimpse a modern-day dinosaur in miniature. Basilisks are normally found near water, for water is their chief escape route. Relying on surface tension, their enormous hind feet, and widely spread toes, they can run across a body of water to safety before they're in any danger of sinking, a technique that has earned them the name of "Jesus Christ Lizard."

One of the other most conspicuous animals at Cahuita is the toucan. Probably no tropical bird is more recognizable, nor more fondly regarded, than this oddly constructed creature. There are six species of toucans in Costa Rica and the two largest—the keel-billed and the chestnut-mandibled—are both common along the southern Caribbean coast.

The first sight of a toucan is an astonishment, as one after another of these giant-billed birds glides across one's path. Their flight is like that of a crippled airplane—leaping off its perch, the toucan spreads its wings in a glide, but immediately begins to sink earthward, and only with a burst of flapping wings does it regain its height, only to start sinking again on the next glide. It is tempting to suggest that the bird is somehow trying to contend with the weight of its massive bill, but this is not the case. The thick, familiar bill of the toucan is extremely light, despite its size, and is no hindrance whatsoever.

The sun can be blisteringly hot along this coast, but on most days the heat is mercifully brief. Dawn is often clear and fresh, but heavy clouds begin to build by midmorning, until under a blackened sky, the afternoon is cooled by a thunderous downpour. The soaking rain travels inland, accompanied by flashes of lightning, until it disappears among the brooding wall of mountains to the southwest—the Talamanca Range.

Left:
A green vine snake begins to devour a frog and will ultimately swallow it whole.

Opposite:
The reflected light from the eyes of the spectacled caiman is often the only sign of their presence.

Overleaf:
Unlike other hummingbirds, which guard flowers within a feeding territory, the long-tailed hermit wanders through the forest in search of nectar.

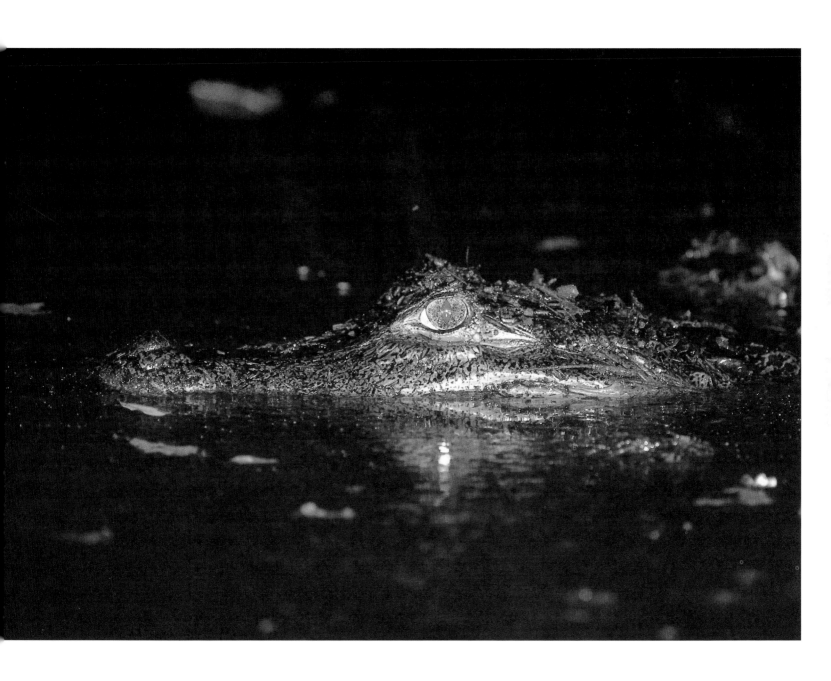

THE FORESTS OF EDEN

THE TALAMANCA RANGE

IT WAS STILL DARK WHEN WE ROSE, THE AIR NEAR FREEZING. Bundling up, we set out on the trail beneath a sky full of stars. At this altitude, the thin air made the walking more difficult, and though we climbed slowly, we were forced to stop every few meters, to rest and catch our breath. The first glow of dawn revealed a jagged line of mountains above us, like a black sawblade against the brightening sky.

After two hours of climbing we reached the final pitch, a hand-over-hand scramble up the last hundred meters to the summit of Chirripó Grande. At 3,820 meters, it is the highest point in Costa Rica. To the east, the sun had already risen over the shimmering Caribbean, more than a hundred kilometers away; in the west, the Pacific still lay in our shadow. In every direction, endless ranges of mountains stretched into the hazy distance, one after another.

This rocky peak is only one of a dozen or more that rise over three thousand meters, forming the tallest mountains in Costa Rica—the Talamanca Range. It is Costa Rica's wildest corner, a landscape little changed from the time of Columbus, who looked up at these mountains five hundred years ago on his final voyage to the New World. Even now, most of the two-hundred-kilometer range is covered in forest, an unbroken blanket of green.

Rugged and inaccessible, the impenetrable valleys of the Talamancas were never occupied by the Conquistadores, and for centuries formed a last redoubt for the indigenous people that once inhabited much of Costa Rica. Even today, most of the country's few remaining native people live here—among them the Bribri, the Guaymi, and the Cabecar—within a series of isolated reserves on either flank of the mountains.

The Talamanca Range was a natural choice for protection within the national park system since it represents the largest roadless area in the country. Over the years, parks and reserves have been added, until today more than 250,000 hectares have been set aside within a unique complex of protected land known as the La Amistad (Friendship) Biosphere Reserve. This is the largest contiguous reserve in all of Central America, connecting the majority of the Talamanca Range, many of the watersheds on either slope, and an adjoining forest wilderness in the Chiriqui Highlands of neighboring Panama.

Because of its size, La Amistad is an unparalleled reservoir of biological wealth, with a range of intact life zones that reaches from the humid lowlands, through rarely intact middle elevations to the high rocky peaks along the Continental Divide. So profound is its scope, in fact, that in 1983 the United Nations designated La Amistad a World Heritage Site, placing it alongside other international treasures such as the Grand Canyon and the great pyramids of Egypt.

The two largest components of the La Amistad Biosphere Reserve are national parks—Chirripó and La Amistad. Although the two are joined along the crest of the Talamanca Range, they could hardly be more dissimilar in character. La Amistad is an immense forested wilderness, a vast sea of trees, while most of Chirripó is above the timberline, as close as Costa Rica comes to a true alpine landscape.

At one time, forest covered almost every corner of Costa Rica, except for a few areas of swamp, grasslands, and along the rocky coast. But trees never colonized the tops of the highest mountains, which were too high and too cold for forests to become established. In their place grew what is known as *paramo*, the open treeless landscape typical of the high plateaus of the Andes, far to the south. For most of Costa Rica, the *paramo* is found only on the windy summits of a few high peaks, like grassy islands in the sky, separated by miles of lowland forests. But in Chirripó National

Park, large areas lie above the timberline, making it the most important area of *paramo* in Central America.

During the Ice Age, these peaks rose high enough for glaciers to form—just nine degrees north of the Equator. Although the ice is gone now, it left behind its characteristic marks on the landscape—sharp peaks, broad ice-carved valleys, and scattered alpine lakes. It is a landscape more akin to the highlands of Scotland than the tropical forests that surround it on every side.

Chirripó has long been popular with hikers and climbers; every year, the high peaks attract thousands of young Costa Ricans, despite the fact that (or perhaps because) climbing them is one of the most challenging physical enterprises in Costa Rica. The route to the high country is a single, grueling trail, climbing some 2,500 meters in seventeen kilometers. It is a singular test of determination; many would-be climbers turn back in exhaustion without ever reaching the *paramo*. Still, every year there is a running race to the summit; this year's winner made the trip up and back in a blistering three hours and seventeen minutes.

The trail to Chirripó begins among the farms and pastures of San Gerardo de Rivas, a tiny village tucked into a narrow valley at the foot of the high peaks. With its bucolic pastures and backdrop of mountains, it is like Switzerland without the snow. From San Gerardo, the trail climbs mercilessly uphill, first through farms and fields, until it finally enters the forest.

The forest grows steadily grander and more lush as the trail gains altitude, and happily, the air cools, making the effort more bearable. The middle elevations of these mountains receive the brunt of the weather off the Pacific and are typically swaddled in clouds by midday, even in the dry season. As a result, they are perpetually damp, the treetops lost in swirling mist.

Ancient gnarled oaks dominate in this cloud forest, their heavy limbs covered in mosses and epiphytes. This is one of the loveliest places in Costa Rica, a magical spot, yet few people who make the climb to Chirripó have the energy to lift their eyes from the trail long enough to enjoy it. Except for the faint sigh of the wind above, and the sound of dripping water, it is an extraordinarily quiet place. Occasionally, though, you may be fortunate to hear a mournful whistle from the misty tangle of limbs overhead, gently repeated over and over. Poised motionless on a thin branch, its long green train waving in the slight breeze, sits a resplendent quetzal.

Tropical forests have no shortage of colorful birds, but the male quetzal is singularly exquisite, a bird of emeralds and rubies. Many people consider it the most beautiful bird in the world. With its blood red breast lined with iridescent green feathers, it is startlingly regal; no surprise that its feathers once adorned the capes of Aztec kings.

The colors of the quetzal are ever-changing—at one moment brilliant green, the next a cold metallic blue—for the iridescent hues are not the result of pigment, but an artifice of the actual structure of its feathers. As with the gem-like brilliance of hummingbirds, the quetzal's feathers reflect different colors depending on the angle of the light that strikes them. One would expect that the quetzal's vivid colors might make it easy to see, but, in fact, the opposite is true. The quetzal knows he is dazzling, and hides his crimson breast by turning his back to any observer. From this angle he shows only his shimmering green, almost invisible in the dappled shadows of the forest canopy. Invariably, the best way to locate a quetzal is by his plaintive call; once heard it is never forgotten.

The quetzal has an almost legendary status in Costa Rica, a fact due as much to marketing as aesthetics. It has become a kind of poster child for the tropical

Opposite, above:

A "fog-bow" arcs over the open paramo in the Chirripo National Park.

Opposite, below:

Cloud forest, Chirripo National Park.

Overleaf:

Columns of basalt lava soften the fall of a small cascade in La Amistad.

rainforest—its bright colors and long tail adorn dozens of brochures and travel guides. So effective has been their promotion that even non-birders go off in search of them with an almost fanatic zeal.

Never widespread, quetzals were originally found in misty highland forests all the way from southern Mexico to western Panama. Today, however, most of these forests are gone, and quetzals survive only in the few scattered remnants. In the vast forests of the Talamanca Range, and the adjoining forest in Panama, the birds still thrive; more quetzals live here than anywhere else on earth.

Climbing higher along the Chirripó trail, the forest becomes even wetter, the moss heavier and thicker on the trees until it seems to cover every inch of bark and branch. Wild bamboo forms impenetrable thickets, where invisible birds chatter. Then, abruptly, the trail emerges from dripping forest into a barren wasteland of blackened trees and stumps. Fires have ravaged much of the upper elevation forests in Chirripó, as well as a large percentage of the *paramo*. In fact, some estimates are that 45 percent of all the *paramo* within the national park has been burned. While a few fires have been due to natural causes, others have almost certainly been started by human hands, either accidentally or deliberately. The most recent fire was in 1992, and the recovery since then has been slow.

Climbing the last major slope—aptly named Repentant's Hill—the trail enters the open country of the *paramo*. A couple of spartan huts lie in the floor of a narrow valley, the base camp for mountain climbers, and a welcome sight after eight hours or more on the trail.

The inevitable giddiness one feels at having reached the top may come from relief at having finished the ordeal, or it may also signal the first effects of altitude sickness. This is not a life-threatening affliction, but it is often a debilitating one, in which even the hardiest of climbers may feel themselves sapped of energy, dehydrated, and unable to sleep, despite their exhaustion.

The paramo is an austere place, with none of the extravagant lushness of the forests below; the diversity of life is very low at this altitude. The most abundant plant is a spiky dwarf bamboo, with thick, coarse leaves that help it retain moisture. There are also surprisingly bright gardens of wildflowers, including some familiar species from the mountains in temperate zones, such as lupine and Indian paintbrush.

The few birds in evidence—the sooty robin, a dark, bold thrush, unafraid of humans, and the little volcano junco, with its odd pale eyes—have somehow learned to adapt to the rigors of life above the timberline. Juncos are common sights inside the rustic trail shelters, where they gather crumbs and scraps left from the previous night's meal. Occasionally a chittering flock of swifts may streak past high overhead, but otherwise, the *paramo* is quiet and devoid of song.

There are a handful of mammals in these highland valleys as well, rabbits and mice and, of course, their predators, coyotes and red-tailed hawks. But these are rarely seen, their presence revealed only by tracks left in a patch of mud along the trail after an afternoon rain.

The most obvious substance throughout the high country is something quite rare in the forest below—rock itself. The rocks of the Talamanca Range are among the oldest and most complex in Costa Rica, yet the mountains that loom so high now did not exist just a few million years ago. This is a young landscape, still growing. Since before the time of the dinosaurs, Central America was little more than a chain of volcanic islands—not unlike the present Aleutians. Ultimately, the collision of crustal plates that formed these volcanoes lifted the Central American isthmus from the sea, joining North and South America together.

Left:

In the middle of a Talamanca stream, a delicate fern grows on a tiny cluster of rocks.

Opposite:

The vaulting prop roots o a strangler fig once squeezed the life from an older host tree, now long since rotted away.

Overleaf:

An acorn woodpecker returns to its cloud forest nest hole.

Up until this time, these two great continents had been separated by open sea, and from a biological point of view, had little in common. Life had evolved on each in isolation, and over the eons, had taken quite different paths. North America had bears, rabbits, horses and, surprisingly, rhinoceros; none of these had existed in the South. South America, on the other hand, had an array of quite different creatures such as monkeys, sloths, and porcupines.

When at last the connection was made, life—never one to miss an opportunity—spread quickly in both directions. The impact was sudden and dramatic. Creatures suddenly confronted others with which they had no experience, and, in some cases, against which they had no defense. Many species became extinct in the millennia that followed; sadly, the American rhino is no more. But other creatures expanded their range and did very well in their new homes. The lowly opossum, for instance, is a southern marsupial that successfully made the trip north and is now happily ensconced virtually throughout North America.

Other animals traveled south and flourished in the tropics; among these were the cats, which were unknown in South America until the land bridge paved the way. Today, Central and South America have no less than six species of native cats, twice as many as we have in North America.

One important factor that affected this successful radiation was that cats moved south into the tropics, where diversity is almost universally greater than in temperate latitudes. There were, simply said, more ways to make a living in this new environment.

Central America, then, is a melting pot, a crossroads of life that today possesses a melange of animals with origins on both continents, north and south. Perhaps no single area along this isthmus

...ungus beetles often ...ather in enormous con-...entrations. Although each ... no bigger than a ladybug, ...ey may cover an entire ...ee trunk in the forest, a ...ehavior that may be ...ocial—or defensive.

is more important to the remaining wildlife of this region than the forests of La Amistad.

The national park that forms the core of La Amistad Biosphere Reserve is the largest in Costa Rica. Few roads approach its boundaries, and only a handful of trails penetrate its vast interior. Perhaps more than any other park in Costa Rica's system, La Amistad is symbolic of the future of national parks, not simply as playgrounds for nature-loving tourists, but as vital reservoirs of life. The day will almost certainly come when every parcel of land outside of parks and preserves will be inhabited, farmed or deforested. When this happens, La Amistad will still be a thriving ecosystem, a living link to the past.

This is true simply because of its size. In general terms, the bigger the park, the better it is—at least for the plants and animals that inhabit it. Animals need a certain amount of space to survive, areas in which they must move to find enough food. For smaller animals, this may mean only a hectare or two, but large animals, especially predators, may need parcels of many square kilometers. In addition, there may be a minimum number of individuals necessary in a contiguous area to constitute a viable, thriving population. If we assume a conservative figure of two hundred animals, it is possible to quickly grasp the problem of saving wildlife. To maintain a healthy population of a certain species may require an area of two thousand square kilometers. Anything less than that, and it is only a matter of time before the species will vanish, from either lack of food, or lack of genetic diversity. Hunting, of course, accelerates this decline and can hasten the final disappearance of a species already on the brink.

Take jaguars, for example. In one forest reserve in Belize, jaguars are thought to exist in densities of about one animal for every sixteen square kilometers. At

that rate, and assuming that jaguars are evenly distributed—which is almost certainly not the case—then there may be only one hundred twenty-five jaguars in all of La Amistad National Park. We don't know for sure, but if it is true, is this a large enough population to be viable over the next decade? The next century?

Although no one knows the answers to these questions, one thing is certain: without extensive wild areas like La Amistad, animals like the jaguar have no future at all.

For that reason, the creation and continued protection of large parks is vital to the survival of these, and many other threatened species. But as human populations continue to grow, the pressure on such wild places can only intensify. Every day it grows more difficult to set aside new areas of land for parks and reserves, or even to find suitable land still intact. In this light, what has been accomplished in Costa Rica seems to have taken place at a crucial moment. Today, only twenty years after the creation of the park system, such a task would be impossible; the vast expanses of forest, including Corcovado, Braulio Carrillo, and La Amistad, would simply not exist.

Left:

A praying mantis hunts among the flowers of a bougainvillea.

Opposite:

A more subtle predator, the leaf-mimic mantis finds a suitable cluster of leaves and simply waits for prey to stray within reach.

Overleaf:

White fungi hasten the decay of a streamside log in La Amistad Biosphere Reserve.

Opposite:

The bright colors of the
amanita mushroom are a
warning of toxicity.

Right:

More than 1,200 species
of orchids have been
found in Costa Rica so far;
others almost certainly
wait for discovery.

AFTERWORD

While Costa Rica has done a remarkable job in protecting her natural areas, few people believe that the task is complete. "The fact is that this country is worse off today, environmentally speaking," says Alvaro Ugalde, "than it was when we started twenty-five years ago. We have lost more soil, the forests are gone, and the rivers are more polluted. If the park system has been successful, and I think it has, it is largely because it forced people to begin thinking about the future."

And what does that future hold? Costa Rica still faces significant economic and environmental problems, not the least of which is a population growth rate that has continued to be one of the highest in the region. Deforestation has slowed in the past few years, but there are still few areas outside of the parks where natural forest remains intact.

Meanwhile, one of the major questions facing the national parks is how, or if, the system should continue to grow. Has everything worth saving been saved? In a study done in 1994, an international team of biologists looked to see how successful the park system has been in protecting a representative sample of Costa Rica's natural ecosystems. They found that while the parks did an excellent job in some areas (the high *paramo* of the Talamanca Range, for example, is essentially 100 percent protected), other ecosystems were woefully underprotected.

Specifically, of the twenty-three defined life zones found in Costa Rica, they found that only seven were adequately protected, with at least a minimum of ten thousand hectares set aside. (Though many biologists believe even this amount is insufficient to protect the majority of species within an ecosystem.) For that reason, one of the continuing goals for the park system is to try to add new areas that may have been overlooked.

It is a daunting task. Some of these habitats essentially no longer exist in a wild state, such as the middle elevation forests that once blanketed the now densely populated Central Valley. There is simply no land left to protect. In other parts of the country, however, there is still hope—if action is taken quickly. In some cases, this may entail the outright purchase of potential parkland, while in other cases it may simply require the upgrading of existing public land held for other uses. One example of these are forest reserves, which like our own national parks are generally protected as timber resources, not for strict conservation purposes.

In addition, there is an ongoing effort to enlarge existing parks, and to connect them, wherever possible, with one another. Mario Boza, in particular, is continuing to devote himself to this task, and not just within Costa Rica. Boza is working to create a green corridor through all of Central America, the Mesoamerican Biological Corridor.

At the same time, there has been a major shift in the management approach to the national parks. The new plan is aimed at decentralizing the entire national park system through the creation of regional "conservation areas." This would place more of the administration and planning functions into local hands. "To have a centralized national parks system is an obsolete idea," Boza explained. "That worked when we created them, but it doesn't work now. We need to give more independence to the conservation areas.

"The idea is that the different conservation areas will have a lot of administrative independence. There will continue to be a small central national parks office in San José, but the day-to-day activity, the development, planning, and administration, will be in the hands of each conservation area."

One compelling reason for this new emphasis on regional control is to ensure the local support for parks and conservation that is so vital to their long-term survival. Although Costa Ricans, by and large, have tremendous pride in, and respect for, their park system, resentment can sometimes develop in local communities when land-use decisions are made by people who do not live in the region affected. The conservation area plan would give local people a voice and a direct hand in issues that will directly affect them. This may prove to be the key to the long-term survival of the national parks.

Ultimately, the challenges that face Costa Rican parks are the same that we all must address in the years and decades ahead. Are wild lands important to us, as well as the creatures that inhabit them? And if so, what must we do to ensure their survival, not simply in the short run, but long into the next millennium? Are we willing to set limits for ourselves in favor of plants and animals that have no voice in their own defense, and for whom we are de facto stewards? These are difficult questions: Costa Rica has committed herself to trying to find the answers.

BIBLIOGRAPHY

Boza, Mario. *Costa Rica National Parks*. Madrid/San Jose: Editorial INCAFO S.A., 1992.
Compiled by one of the founders of the national park system, this book provides an illustrated survey of all the parks and reserves in Costa Rica.

Dressler, Robert L. *Field Guide to the Orchids of Costa Rica and Panama*. Ithaca, NY: Comstock/Cornell, 1993.
Comstock/Cornell, Ithaca, 1993.
The most complete field guide available to the orchids of Costa Rica. However, field identification is very technical, and this book can be tough going for the nonspecialist.

Forsyth, Adrian, and Ken Miyata. *Tropical Nature*. New York: Scribner's, 1984.
A quite wonderful book, eminently readable, about the endless diversity of the tropical forests by two talented writers and biologists. This was the first book I read about tropical ecosystems and it remains the best; in some ways it inspired this volume.

Janzen, Daniel H. *Costa Rican Natural History*. Chicago: University of Chicago Press, 1983.
The bible of biological reference books on Costa Rica, with articles by 174 contributors, covering basic natural history of a large number of the plants and animals, as well as broader topics of climate, geology, and biogeography.

Stiles, Gary F., and Alexander Skutch. *A Guide to the Birds of Costa Rica*. Illustrations by Dana Gardner. Ithaca, NY: Cornell University Press, 1989.
The essential guide to the more than eight hundred species of birds in Costa Rica. Not inexpensive, and weighing several pounds, it is nonetheless a wonderful companion, crammed with information.

Wallace, David Rains. *The Quetzal and the Macaw*. San Francisco: Sierra Club Books, 1992.
An excellent, detailed history of the development of the Costa Rican national park system, with extensive interviews with the key figures in its history.